Picture Puzzles FOR DUMMIES®

by Elizabeth J. Cárdenas-Nelson
and Jennifer Connolly

Wiley Publishing, Inc.

Picture Puzzles For Dummies®

Published by
Wiley Publishing, Inc.
111 River St.
Hoboken, NJ 07030-5774
www.wiley.com

Published by Wiley Publishing, Inc., Indianapolis, Indiana

Published simultaneously in Canada

For general information on our other products and services, please contact our Customer Care Department within the U.S. at 877-762-2974, outside the U.S. at 317-572-3993, or fax 317-572-4002.

For technical support, please visit www.wiley.com/techsupport.

Wiley also publishes its books in a variety of electronic formats. Some content that appears in print may not be available in electronic books.

Library of Congress Control Number: 2009933369

ISBN: 978-0-470-50685-1

Manufactured in the United States of America

10 9 8 7 6 5 4 3 2

About the Authors

Elizabeth J. Cárdenas-Nelson: Elizabeth received a bachelor's degree in Fine Arts from Cleveland State University. An avid advocate of using computers and computer programs as the modern artist's brush and canvas, Elizabeth has extensive experience in design, layout, and illustration and has taught instructional classes on Adobe Photoshop. She also contributed to *Photoshop CS2 Visual Encyclopedia* (Wiley). Spending a large chunk of her Sundays working puzzles and unable to travel without a puzzle book in her backpack, Elizabeth is a devoted puzzler.

Jennifer Connolly: Jennifer has a passion for research and writing, which led to a career as a professional editor and author. Her family of avid puzzlers got her hooked on puzzles at an early age, and Jennifer continues to stash puzzle books in her car, purse, and kids' tote bags so that she can work a puzzle at any given moment.

Dedication

Elizabeth: To my husband, Dave N., who supports my every endeavor.

Jennifer: To the people I love more than puzzles — David, my husband, and my two daughters, Hannah and Ella.

Authors' Acknowledgments

Elizabeth: I am so thankful that Lindsay Lefevere, my Acquisitions Editor at Wiley, remembered me and my love of Photoshop and asked me to do this book. I appreciate that she partnered me with Jennifer Connolly, my co-author. Jennifer provided great captions and ideas for solving puzzles, and her encouragement, great sense of fun, and even nature — no matter how crazy or hectic the project seemed to be getting — helped make this project run smoothly. I also wish to thank all the people who contributed photographs, giving me an endless array of fun and distinct choices for puzzles in the book. Certainly I owe more than thanks to my husband, Dave, for making and providing many meals so that I could work without distraction. Additionally, thanks to Dave, Julie Conlin, and Karen Kuhlman for testing the puzzles. Last, but certainly not least, thanks go to Kelly Ewing for maintaining the vision of the book and keeping the project on track.

Jennifer: I certainly appreciate the opportunity that Lindsay Lefevere, my Acquisitions Editor at Wiley, gave to me, and I can't thank her enough for bringing me on board to write on such a fun topic. And many thanks goes out to my Project Editor, Kelly Ewing. She was wonderfully easy to work with, and she made the process effortless and painless. However, this book wouldn't be a book without the huge effort of my co-author, Elizabeth Cardenas-Nelson. Elizabeth dedicated a great amount of time and attention to the puzzles, was so easy to work with, and from the start was an all-around great partner on this project. I certainly could not have done my part without her or without the help of David Connolly, my husband. David made sure I always had the time that I needed to get my writing done, and he proved to be a huge help whenever I felt "stuck." Of course, my girls helped a lot, too, both by sleeping so well at night that I had enough time to get my writing done as well as providing comic relief whenever I needed it — sometimes, even when I didn't realize that I needed it. And last, but certainly not least, I must thank my family full of puzzlers, especially my mom, Linda Murphy, for introducing me to the wonderful world of puzzling. I now always have something to do in the waiting room or the airplane or anywhere.

Publisher's Acknowledgments

We're proud of this book; please send us your comments through our Dummies online registration form located at http://dummies.custhelp.com. For other comments, please contact our Customer Care Department within the U.S. at 877-762-2974, outside the U.S. at 317-572-3993, or fax 317-572-4002.

Some of the people who helped bring this book to market include the following:

Acquisitions, Editorial, and Media Development

Project Editor: Kelly Ewing

Acquisitions Editor: Lindsay Sandman Lefevere

Assistant Editor: Erin Calligan Mooney

Editorial Program Coordinator: Joe Niesen

General Reviewer: David W. Fisher (http://puzzles.about.com)

Senior Editorial Manager: Jennifer Ehrlich

Editorial Supervisor and Reprint Editor: Carmen Krikorian

Editorial Assistant: David Lutton, Jennette ElNaggar

Art Coordinator: Alicia B. South

Cover Photos: Front: Kevin Kirschner; Back: Elizabeth Cárdenas-Nelson

Cartoons: Rich Tennant (www.the5thwave.com)

Composition Services

Project Coordinator: Lynsey Stanford

Layout and Graphics: Laura Campbell, Brooke C. Graczyk, Erin Zeltner

Proofreaders: John Greenough, Melanie Hoffman, Jennifer Theriot

---

Publishing and Editorial for Consumer Dummies

Diane Graves Steele, Vice President and Publisher, Consumer Dummies

Kristin Ferguson-Wagstaffe, Product Development Director, Consumer Dummies

Ensley Eikenburg, Associate Publisher, Travel

Kelly Regan, Editorial Director, Travel

Publishing for Technology Dummies

Andy Cummings, Vice President and Publisher, Dummies Technology/General User

Composition Services

Debbie Stailey, Director of Composition Services

Table of Contents

Part IV: The Part of Tens 173

Chapter 2: Ten Tips for Solving 175

Chapter 3: Ten Ways to Build Your Brain for Better Solving 181

Introduction

Picture puzzles make up a matchless niche in the puzzling world. Because each picture is unique, *Picture Puzzles For Dummies* offers limitless types of puzzles and endless arrangements that present one-of-a-kind puzzles on every page. Unlike traditional word or number puzzles, *Picture Puzzles For Dummies* launches you into a festive, full-color dimension of puzzling, challenging you to discover differences or similarities between pictures or pieces of a picture.

About This Book

Picture Puzzles For Dummies promises a great adventure, steering you through a variety of puzzles of varying levels of difficulty. Whether you're a novice or expert puzzler, you can find plenty of puzzles in this book to scratch your puzzling itch.

Although you're sure to enjoy each and every puzzle in this book, this book is set up so that you can move freely from one chapter or part to another. For example, you may dive right in to solving puzzles but then get stuck and want some ideas on solving picture puzzles. You can just stop what you're doing and flip to Chapter 1 or the Part of Tens in the back of this book to get the info you need on solving. Better yet, we won't even make you read the entire chapter. If you find a section or set of sections that you're interested in, feel free to read just those parts, although if you want to take full advantage of all of the ideas on better solving practices, you may want to read it all. But we're biased, of course.

Conventions Used in This Book

To make navigating this book even easier, we include some special conventions:

- **Names of puzzle types:** We include three different types of puzzles in this book, and we don't want you to be confused about how they're named. Here's how they break down:
  - **Spot the changes:** Puzzles of this type include two seemingly identical pictures with subtle changes made that you have to find.

    - **One of these is not like the other:** This puzzle type lists several seemingly identical pictures, but you have to spot the one that contains one difference from the others.
    - **Cut-ups:** You can identify this puzzle because it looks like a jigsaw puzzle on paper.

- **Number of changes:** For each spot-the-changes puzzle, we identify the number of changes contained in the puzzle.
- **Grid numbers:** For spot-the-changes puzzles, a grid with numbers and letters surrounds the puzzles. The grid helps you solve because you can use it as a guide, but it also helps you identify changes in the solution.
- **Cut-up grid:** For each cut-up puzzle, we give you a grid as well as one piece filled in to get you started.
- **Solutions:** Each puzzle type has a unique presentation for its solution:
    - **Spot the changes:** Because it can be difficult to actually recognize the change if you haven't spotted it, we give you the grid number followed by a description of the change.
    - **One of these is not like the other:** We circle the one difference to clearly show you the solution for this puzzle type.
    - **Cut-ups:** Perhaps the easiest solution to review, the cut-up solution simply shows the pieced-together picture.

What You're Not to Read

Although we like every bit of this book, you can definitely skip over some parts without missing anything. You may encounter gray boxes, called sidebars, which include interesting information about puzzling. If you want to skip over these sidebars, you won't have a problem understanding how to solve picture puzzles or even solving the ones in this book. These boxes simply contain things *we* find interesting about picture puzzles, and while we certainly would be flattered if you thought so, too, we'll never know if you skip them.

Foolish Assumptions

As we wrote this book, we had to make a few assumptions about you, and here's what we thought:

- **You may have no or limited experience with picture puzzles.** Although you may enjoy puzzling, we realize that you may not be all that familiar with picture puzzles. So we've not only included puzzles at beginner levels, but we've also included plenty of information on getting started.

- **You may have significant picture puzzle experience.** So you're an old pro, huh? Well, we have plenty of action for you, too. We have several levels of puzzles that can tempt even the most experienced puzzler.
- **You want to know more about solving picture puzzles.** Not only can you find chapters full of tips and ideas on solving picture puzzles, but also, you can put them to practice on a variety of puzzles included in this book.

How This Book Is Organized

We've put this book together in parts and chapters so that you can easily find information on solving puzzles, puzzles to solve, and the solutions. The following sections list the different parts and what those parts include so that you can easily navigate your way through this book.

Part I: Picking Apart Picture Puzzles

This part describes the types of picture puzzles we include in this book. It also offers great ideas for solving them, as well as how solving picture puzzles can benefit your brain.

Part II: Progressing through the Puzzles

Come to Part II to discover the fantastic world of picture puzzles. We include puzzles of all levels of difficulty, with plenty of variety, in this part. Whether you want to start out with some easy puzzles, try your hand at something tricky, or dive right into the more diabolical puzzles, you're sure to find a puzzle that will please you in this part. Note the use of black and white in the Bewildering section was intentional.

Part III: Checking Your Work — No Peeking!

Watch yourself now! As tempting as it may be, you don't want to step foot into this part unless you've solved a puzzle. Trust us: You'll be disappointed when you peek into this part to find out a solution that you couldn't solve. So try your best to work through the puzzle first, and if you do get stuck, check out Chapter 1 or the Part of Tens before you seek out the solution. Save this part solely for checking the puzzles you've solved.

Part IV: The Part of Tens

The Part of Tens includes two chapters created in a top ten–list format. In this part, you can find tips on solving picture puzzles, as well as ideas on how to train your brain to solve puzzles better and quicker.

Icons Used in This Book

To make picking out information from the book even easier, we include some icons to flag specific information.

The Tip icon lets you know when you're about to read information that can make you a smarter and savvier solver.

Just as this icon indicates, you don't want to forget any information that this icon flags.

Look out! When you come across this icon, it warns you against doing things that may be detrimental!

Where to Go from Here

You want to dive right in, but are you ready for the deep end of diabolical puzzles, or do you need to wade through the kiddie pool of easy puzzles first? Well, that depends on how confident you are at solving picture puzzles. If you think you've got picture puzzles pretty much licked, step on up to the tricky or tough puzzles and give 'em a try. If they're too difficult, step it down a notch, but if you breeze right through them, take it up to the next level. Now if you're confident that you're a beginner, head on over to the easy puzzles, and work your way through a few. When you feel confident that you can easily cut through them, try the next level, and so on, until you come across a real challenge.

If you're brand new to picture puzzles, head directly to Chapter 1 and find out more about the puzzles as well as strategies to solve them. In fact, you may even benefit from reading the Part of Tens as well to give your solving skills some extra oomph. Just remember, it doesn't matter where you begin because you can always move back and forth as you quickly solve puzzles or face real challenges.

Part I

Picking Apart Picture Puzzles

In this part . . .

This part introduces you to the world of picture puzzles and helps you get started. In Chapter 1, you can discover the different types of picture puzzles contained in this book as well as understand how they function. Chapter 1 also provides you with several options for solving picture puzzles and tells you how puzzling can boost your brain power.

Chapter 1

Getting Set to Solve Picture Puzzles

In This Chapter

- Figuring out the puzzle types
- Solving puzzles with specific strategies
- Engaging your brain with picture puzzles

Whether you've just become interested in pictures puzzles or you've tried some already and need tips on solving them, you can find all the information you need in this chapter. No matter what section you read in this chapter — whether you get familiar with puzzle types, solving strategies, or ways to boost your brain — each section gives you some info that can make you stronger at solving the picture puzzles in this book.

In this chapter, we explain how all the puzzle types differ and how breaking them down actually helps get you started on solving them. The more that you're familiar with the type of puzzle you're solving, the better you'll be at solving it. Of course, you probably want to try the solving strategies we describe in this chapter as well. We give you the best strategies that you can use to solve all types of picture puzzles. We even give you ideas on how to boost your brainpower to take your solving skills to the next level.

Getting a Feel for the Picture Puzzle Types

In the wide world of picture puzzles, you run across more than just one type to solve. Each type provides you with a different challenge, and before you dive into solving any puzzle, getting the lay of the land helps you become familiar with how the puzzle works. In the following sections, we describe the three types of puzzles you can solve in this book.

Checking out changes

Spot-the-changes puzzles tend to be the type of picture puzzle most people recognize. In a spot-the-changes puzzle, you're given two pictures that *look* identical at first glance. However, one of the pictures contains some differences — for example, the flower pot in one picture may be blue but green in the other picture'. Although glancing through the puzzle can be an effective strategy while solving, you also need to look closely to pick out all the changes. (See the section later in this chapter, "Solving All Types of Picture Puzzles," for more on solving spot-the-changes puzzles.)

In this book, we let you know how many changes you should be spotting, plus we give you checkboxes so that you can keep track of how many you uncover. (See Chapter 2 for more on how it helps to keep track of your work.) In each puzzle, one of the pictures also has numbers across the top and letters down the side so that you can work the puzzle like a grid, going from section A1 to A2, and so on.

Knowing which one is not like the other

Similar to spot-the-changes puzzles, a one-of-these-is-not-like-the-other puzzle — or a Not puzzle — contains several pictures that all seem to be the same. But unlike the spot-the-changes puzzle, a Not puzzle contains *six* pictures, only *one* of which is slightly different! You have to scour each picture to figure out which one contains a subtle change.

Most people think that Not puzzles must be more difficult than spot-the-changes puzzles, but depending on how easily you can spot a change, a Not puzzle may actually be easier because you're looking for just one change. For some people, finding just one change becomes more of a challenge.

Working a jigsaw puzzle . . . on paper

Regardless of whether you like jigsaw puzzles, you should try cut-up puzzles. Cut-up puzzles consist of two grids: One grid displays a picture divided into numbered pieces, which are scrambled, and the other grid is blank except for one piece, which is correctly placed as a hint to help get you started. You have to figure out where to place each of the other numbered pieces within the grid to make a complete picture.

Sketch or write the numbers of each piece in the empty grid. Sketching can help you as you solve, and writing in the numbers helps keep track of your work. (See the section later in this chapter, "Piecing the picture together," for more on solving cut-up puzzles. See Chapter 2 for more on how keeping track of your work helps you solve the puzzle.)

Serving Up Solving Strategies

You can use several different strategies for solving picture puzzles, and we encourage you to try them all to see which ones work well for you. Not all strategies are puzzle-specific. What works for a spot-the-changes puzzle may also work for a cut-up puzzle. Which ones you decide to use depends largely on which strategies you feel most comfortable with.

Create a solving routine by using a pattern to go over the puzzle or by combining several solving techniques. (See the section "Move through the puzzle in a pattern," later in this chapter, for more on using patterns.) Using a solving routine ensures that you exhaust every technique that works for you and that you scour every nook and cranny of the puzzle while you're solving. For more on solving routines, see Chapter 2. Just remember: You won't find an exact step-by-step routine in this book because whatever solving routine works for you may not work for someone else. So try all the techniques to find out which routines result in solving success for you.

You can use any of the strategies listed in the following sections for any puzzle type in this book. However, we break the puzzle-solving strategies down by puzzle type in the following sections. By searching the solving strategies by puzzle type, you can see which strategies work best for each type. Then it's up to you to overlap strategies and experiment with any of them to find the best solving routine for you.

Spotting the differences

In spot-the-changes puzzles, your job is to, well, spot the changes. Sounds easy enough until you find all of them except two, which results in chaos. Why chaos? First, you discover that you can't put the book down until you find the two changes that you're missing. Then, supper begins burning in the oven and boiling over on the stove. Your boss calls you about work, and you can't take your mind off of the puzzle to answer the phone. Your kids need a bath because they've been playing in the mud while you've been trying to solve a picture puzzle. The FedEx guy keeps ringing your doorbell to have you sign for a package, but you don't answer. You want to call out for help from your partner, but you can't do anything until you find those two changes! Chaos.

But if you have a plan — a strategy — before you begin, your searching can easily result in success, and you can avoid the chaos and calamity that fruitless searching brings. Just try using the ideas listed in the following sections to find all the differences in spot-the-changes puzzles.

Look for the obvious

You may think that we've given you an obvious idea. However, in your anxiety to find changes, you may skip over some obvious differences. Follow these two basic strategies to make sure that you don't miss a thing:

- **Glance through the puzzle.** Sounds a bit casual, we know. But when you first begin the puzzle, you can often glance through it and find some pretty obvious differences. A teeny tiny moon that becomes twice its size in the second picture can be pretty obvious, even at a glance.

  Although this technique is most effective when beginning a puzzle, it sure does help when you're stuck, too. Often, when you're stuck, just glancing through the puzzle may help you spot a section, detail, or change that you glossed over earlier.
- **Distinguish the details.** When solving a picture puzzle, a flower isn't a flower. A flower may be a long-stemmed red rose. A tree isn't just a tree. A tree may be a short white birch. If you look at a puzzle and think, "There's a fence," instead of, "There's a wire fence with three posts," you may miss that one of the fence posts has been shortened or is altogether missing.

Move through the puzzle in a pattern

When you use a pattern to search through a puzzle, you discipline yourself to scan the puzzle systematically. Using a systematic approach, you can be sure of the following:

- **You search each space.** A pattern helps you search through each grid space (such as, A1, B1, and so on) with the comfort of knowing you're tackling each piece of the puzzle and not glossing over anything.
- **You search each space thoroughly.** When you search through the puzzle in a pattern, you have a better chance of leaving no stone unturned. By breaking the puzzle up into smaller pieces, you have an easier time looking for minute details
- **You search each space thoroughly while also looking for the obvious.** When you use patterns in conjunction with techniques for finding obvious changes (see the earlier section, "Look for the obvious," for more about searching for the obvious), you tackle both the obvious changes and details in a systematic approach. Although you may glance over the puzzle and then tackle it using a pattern, you still need to distinguish the details and be on the lookout for obvious things you may have missed earlier.

Using a pattern with spot-the-changes puzzles is easy. You study each grid space, comparing it to the other picture's same grid space, and you really have two options:

- **Scan from top to bottom.** Because you have a grid to work with, you begin with A1, then B1, then C1, and so on until you get to the bottom of the puzzle. Then you go back to the top and scour A2, then B2, and so on.
- **Look from left to right.** Using the grid, you work through the puzzle like reading — left to right. Start with A1, then A2, then A3 and so on until you reach the end of the row. Then you begin with B1, then B2, and so on.

Eyeing the oddball

The one-of-these-is-not-like-the-other puzzles — or Not puzzles — don't have grids or other helpers to get you started. You have your peepers and a pencil, perhaps, but that's about it. Such a predicament may scare some people away, but oddly enough, although Not puzzles can pose a challenge, even beginners can solve them.

For some people, having several pictures to compare poses an easier mental challenge than just having two pictures to compare. Of course, more pictures also means more chances that you may miss something. But in the sections that follow, we provide you with some great ideas on solving Not puzzles so that you don't overlook any details.

Keep comparisons focused with a pattern

Using a pattern — a systematic approach — helps you move through the puzzle without missing any details. Not puzzles don't have grids like spot-the-changes puzzles, so you can't use the grid to break down each picture for comparison. However, you can make your own breakdown and still use a pattern. Use these ideas to get you thinking about how you can establish a pattern for solving different Not puzzles:

- **If people are in the picture:** Compare each person from head to toe. You won't get very far if you compare the eyes in one picture to the eyes in another and then skip to comparing the color of the stripes in that person's shirt. Even if you think the detail is the same in all the pictures, still check. After you're sure that you've compared where a person's hair is parted, move on to the color of the hair, and then on to the color of the eyes, and so on.
- **If several objects are in the picture:** Pick specific objects to compare in each picture. The easiest way to compare objects is to move through the photo from left to right, top to bottom.

- **If just one main object is in the picture:** You may feel overwhelmed to see just a single object in a Not puzzle, but just take a deep breath and start at the beginning with the details, literally. Every object, no matter how simple it looks at first, contains multiple elements. For example, if the image is a staircase, compare the details from the top of the staircase to the bottom. Or begin with railing, move on to the steps, and so on. If the image doesn't have an obvious beginning or end (like a wheel or flower), try comparing specific details, such as color, size of things within the image, and so on, moving in a patterned fashion over the image, such as right to left, top to bottom.

Pick out differences in the details

Although you may get lucky and see an obvious difference right at the start, chances are you have to pick through the details to find the one change amongst all of the pictures. But with six pictures to go through, whether you use a pattern or not, you can go a little crazy comparing them all. So use the following ideas to help make sifting through the details less painful:

- **Use one picture as a "base."** Use the first picture in the Not puzzle as your base — the picture you compare all other pictures against. Use a pattern, and then compare the details of the base picture against each of the other pictures. (See the earlier section, "Keep comparisons focused with a pattern," for more on patterns.)
- **Compare details individually.** You may think that you've noticed a particular detail, such as the color of a person's eyes, while comparing another detail, but don't fool yourself. You need to look and compare each detail individually; don't dismiss any detail if you haven't purposefully searched for it and compared it to all the pictures.

Piecing the picture together

Think of cut-up puzzles like a jigsaw puzzle — you have to piece it together with just your eyes . . . unless, of course, you cut the picture out of the book and piece it together on the table, but what's the fun in that? Of course, with no corner pieces let alone a box lid to start with, you may be wondering how you're supposed to begin — let alone solve — this kind of puzzle. Well, we start you off with one piece correctly placed, but the rest is up to you. So check out the following sections to get some ideas on how to finish solving a Not puzzle.

Get a quick take on what the picture is

First, try giving the pieces a quick scan and see whether you can figure out what the picture is. Is it a flower? Is it a beach scene? Is it a garden? You get the idea.

However, you may have a difficult time figuring out what in the world you've been staring at for the past ten minutes. If you find yourself in that predicament, try figuring out what the picture is composed of. Does it look like it has a clump of trees? Can you see the makings of a dirt road?

After you begin to discover what parts make up the entire picture, you can get a better idea on what the picture is as a whole. And after you know what you're looking at, you can begin putting the pieces together.

Especially with some of the more difficult puzzles, you may never figure out what the entire picture is, and that's okay. Even if you're truly stumped, if you can find just one obvious part, you can begin to piece the picture together.

Plug in the obvious parts

Use the process of elimination to piece together obvious parts, leaving the other — often more difficult — pieces for last. For example, if you find the side of a building, try plugging all the pieces together to complete the side of the building and then see what pieces you have leftover. You'll be amazed at how quickly some of the more difficult details fall into place. If you're still stuck on some difficult details, check out the following section, "Leave the difficult details for last."

Even if you don't know exactly where in the grid you should place the obvious parts, still piece it together — in your head, at least. By eliminating the pieces that make up the obvious part you've discovered, you may have an easier time both figuring out where in the grid to place part, as well as where to plug in the finishing details.

Leave the difficult details for last

After you've plugged in some obvious parts, even just a couple of details can still stump you, but you can still solve the cut-up puzzle if you try the following ideas:

- **Look for similarities.** After you put together some obvious parts, look for similarities in those parts that can connect them to your leftover pieces. Check to see whether your leftover pieces share a similar color, background, or setting.
- **Compare empty spots and their borders in the grid.** Find empty spots on the grid and then check out what borders those empty spaces. Check to see whether any lines, colors, or forms on the borders of empty spaces can possibly connect to one of your leftover pieces.
- **Sketch your heart out.** Although you may not be an award-winning artist, you can probably connect some lines or dots. So remember: You don't have to replicate a piece perfectly to figure out where it fits. If you can't figure out by eye what empty spots the leftover pieces can fit into, try sketching it out a bit.

Pumping Mental Iron with Picture Puzzles

Just by carrying this book around, you may find yourself being asked to help solve a neighbor's crossword puzzle or a friend's brainteaser. Because it takes a detail-oriented individual with impeccable focus to solve picture puzzles, people just assume that you've got those skills if they catch you fiddling with picture puzzles.

Regardless where you fall on the mental fitness meter, you not only can solve picture puzzles, but you can also boost your brain power at the same time. Anyone can do pictures puzzles, and everyone can benefit from solving them. Think of solving picture puzzles as a way to maintain as well as increase your mental activity.

The following sections show you how you can get a brain boost from solving picture puzzles, and you can also discover how to take your solving skills to the next level.

Breaking a sweat with your brain

If you don't think you fit the big-brain category — despite what your friends and family believe — start solving picture puzzles and see what differences you discover in your mind, attention, and stress level. In case you can't wait to find out, here's how solving picture puzzles can benefit your brain and body:

- **Muscling up your mind:** Simply put, use it or lose it! Stop staring at the back of headrests on airplanes and work a picture puzzle instead. Take this book with you to your porch and give your mind a mental workout rather than veg out watching the flowers grow.

  Using your mind helps retain mental acuity — the stuff you want when you're older so that you can remember that your keys are on the hook and your glasses aren't misplaced, they're just on your head. Even just a few picture puzzles a day can help you keep your wits about you.

- **Training your attention:** You may think, or have been told by your mother, your teacher, or your spouse, that you don't pay attention. Perhaps that's keeping you from trying picture puzzles, but that complaint should be the reason you work them! Working picture puzzles helps to increase your attention span because you have to remain focused.

Solving a picture puzzle, no matter what type, requires strong focus. You have to be able to block out distractions and keep track of what you've done all while life's distractions attempt to interrupt your focus. Of course, as you learn to be better focused, it may result in your being able to block out your mother, teacher, or spouse more effectively, too. You have to decide whether that's an added bonus or not.

- **Reducing tension:** Just like working out your body can relieve stress, working out your mind can have the same result. Solving some picture puzzles gives you a feeling of success and helps you see the problems that are stressing you from a different perspective.

  Working puzzles give you a simple break as well. Even if you don't solve a puzzle completely, just immersing yourself in something different gives you a break from dwelling on a stressful situation.

Taking it to the next level

Perhaps you understand that picture puzzles give your brain a workout for the better (if you don't understand that, you should check out the earlier section, "Breaking a sweat with your brain"), but you want to boost your solving as well as brain building efforts. You can uncover some ways to take your skills to the next level:

- **Keep your brain challenged.** If you keep your brain challenged, you can better solve puzzles, boost your brainpower, and solve even bigger puzzles. But you have to know when you need to be challenged. Your first clue should be when you breeze through a certain level of picture puzzles. When you burn through solving several puzzles at one sitting, you need to turn up the heat rather than revel in how bright you are.

  To keep your brain challenged:

  - Try a different type of picture puzzle.
  - Move on to a higher level of difficulty.
  - Switch gears to a brain teaser, crossword, or other type of puzzle.

- **Turn off the tube.** Just like your mother told you, television rots your brain. Okay, maybe TV isn't really that bad, but it certainly doesn't help you take your solving skills to the next level. Television increases the chance that you'll eat more and exercise less. And if that wasn't enough, all those commercials are enough to convince you that you don't have it all but that you *do* need it all, which is enough to stress you out (and then make you eat more, exercise less, you get the picture). So do yourself a favor and turn your brain on by turning your TV off!

- **Work out your body to boost brain power.** Although we don't plan on putting you on a strict exercise regimen to increase your ability to solve picture puzzles, we do want to point out that physical activity results in a positive push for brain power. While we'd love to have you sit and work every puzzle in this book (and we hope you do solve every puzzle), you do have to get up and get moving each day. Physical exercise protects the brain and gets your blood flowing and pumping to your brain.

  Go for a walk or give or whatever physical activity you enjoy a try. You can build a better memory and increase your problem-solving skills in the process. And those problem-solving skills come in handy for solving picture puzzles!

Use your brain before you buy

Amidst parental complaints that electronic devices, such as computers and video games, are wasting their kids' time, the industry has answered by touting new — and often expensive — alternatives. Okay, perhaps we're using the word "alternatives" loosely. Basically, the "new alternatives" consist of the exact same products they were selling before: computer and video games, except these games are supposed to help increase brainpower. In fact, you can find ads all over the place that claim their new-fangled electronic games are the best way to build your brain. Of course, you have to turn over more than a few bucks to build your brain with these new toys.

Part II

Progressing through the Puzzles

"I guess you could say I'm almost becoming addicted to these 'spot-the-changes' puzzles."

In this part . . .

If you're ready to try out a puzzle, then this part is for you. You can choose not only from a variety of puzzles — spot the changes, one of these is not like the other, and cut-ups — but also from a variety of difficulty levels. Whether you're a long-time picture puzzler, brand-new beginner, or somewhere between the two, you can find several puzzles and difficulty levels that will continue to interest and challenge you.

Puzzle 1: Easy, Breezy, Beautiful

Don't relax too much in the island life as you try piecing this palm scene together.

©Elizabeth Cárdenas-Nelson

KEEP TRACK

Puzzle 2: Buyer Beware!

Hats off to you (and definitely *this* guy!), if you can catch the changes in this puzzle.

Easy

A

B

C

D

E

1 2 3 4 5

Keep Track

9 Changes

Easy

Puzzle 3: Slip into Something Comfortable

Slide on your favorite slippers and find a cozy spot to plod through all the patterns in this puzzle.

©istockphoto.com/Xavi Arnau

A B C D E

1 2 3 4 5

Keep Track

8 Changes

○ ○ ○ ○ ○ ○ ○ ○

Puzzle 4: Home on the Range

"Keep grazing guys. Just look natural for the tourists. Great job! Wait — who's sitting down on the job back there?"

©Elizabeth Cárdenas-Nelson

Easy

Keep Track

8 Changes

Puzzle 5: A Trendy Spot for a Trim

A salon so comfy and quiet . . . the perfect place to do puzzles!

A
B
C
D
E

1 2 3 4 5

Keep Track

7 Changes

Puzzle 6: Con-grad-ulations!

Don't be distracted by all the pomp and circumstance — you shouldn't graduate to the harder puzzles if you can't find all the changes here!

©Tracy Conlin

A

B

C

D

E

1 2 3 4 5

Keep Track

7 Changes

Easy

Puzzle 7: Kickin' Back on the Beach

Don't get caught up people-watching and miss any of the changes in this puzzle!

©Elizabeth Cárdenas-Nelson

A

B

C

D

E

1 2 3 4 5

Keep Track

7 Changes

Puzzle 8: Here Kitty, Kitty!

It may take a bit of cat and mouse, but you'll eventually piece together this puzzle.

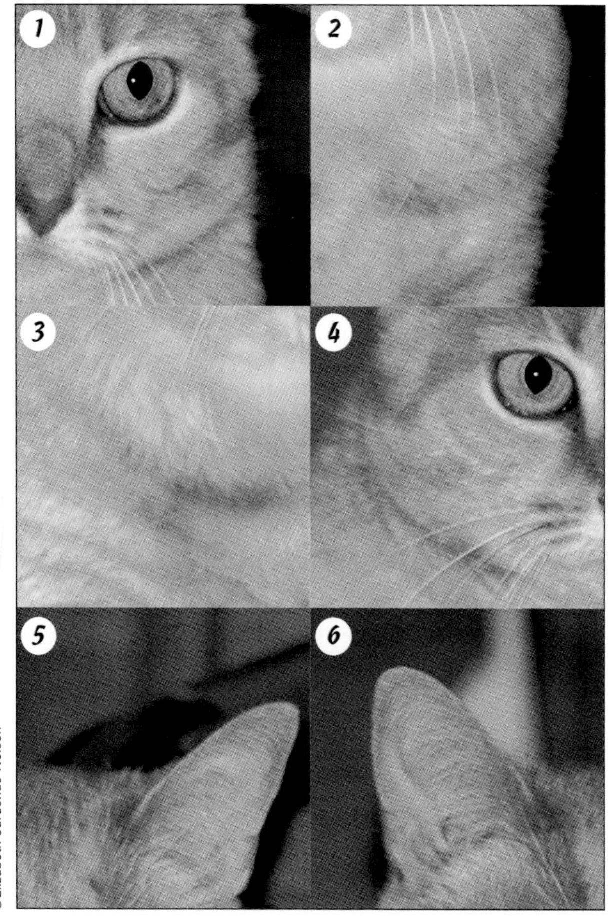

©Elizabeth Cárdenas-Nelson

KEEP TRACK

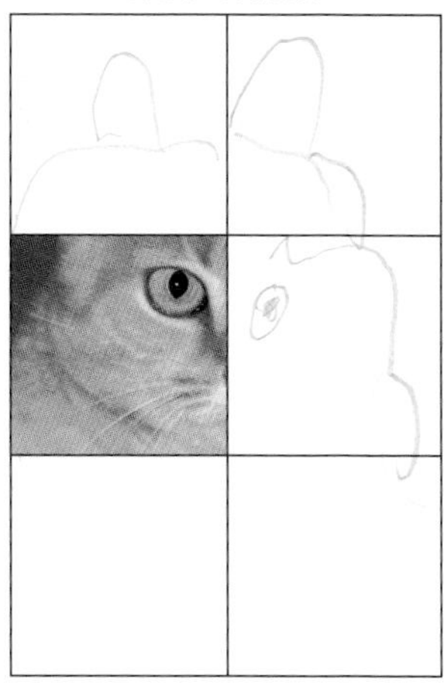

Puzzle 9: Undercover Café

Bright, patterned umbrellas against the brilliant colors conceal the many changes in this puzzle.

©istockphoto.com/Stephen D. Kramer

Easy

A

B

C

D

E

1 2 3 4 5

Keep Track

11 Changes

Puzzle 10: Wrap It up!

Don't get yourself tied into knots over the "presents" of all the changes in this puzzle.

A

B

C

D

E

1 2 3 4 5

Keep Track

8 Changes

Puzzle 11: Float Like a Butterfly

Sting like a bee with your solving skills by spotting the one photo that's different.

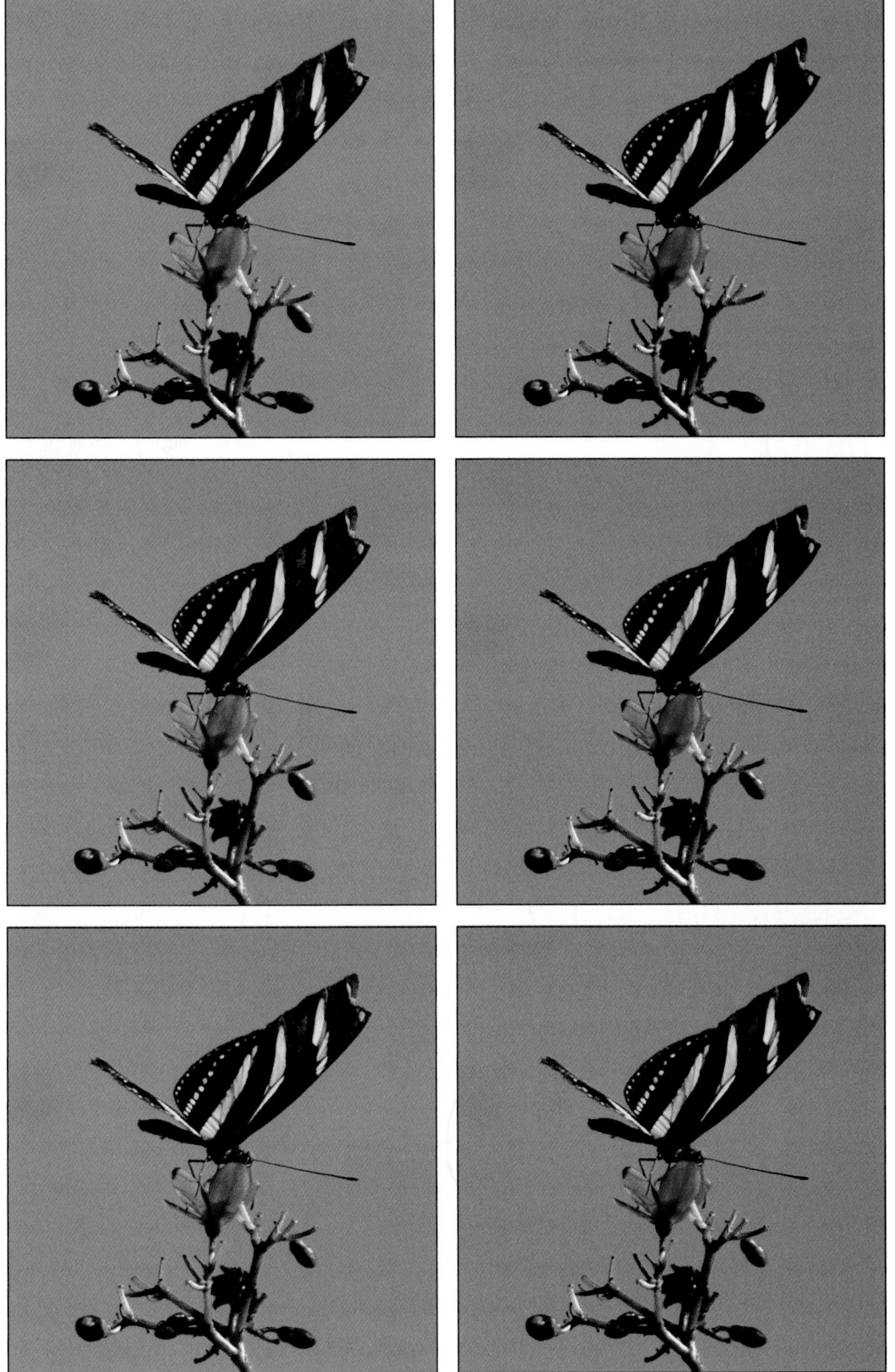

Easy

Puzzle 12: Hats off to the Ladies!

Proof that women *are* better drivers than men.

©Julie Conlin

A

B

C

D

E

1 2 3 4 5

Keep Track

11 Changes

○ ○ ○ ○ ○ ○ ○ ○ ○ ○ ○

Puzzle 13: Oil Can!!

Recycling apparently means different things to different people.

©Sara Kuhlman

A

B

C

D

E

1 2 3 4 5

Easy

Keep Track

10 Changes

Easy

Puzzle 14: A Royal Pair

You can have a ball spotting changes with these two belles.

©Lindsay Lefevere

Keep Track

8 Changes

○ ○ ○ ○ ○ ○ ○ ○

A B C D E

1 2 3 4 5

Puzzle 15: Furry Valentine

You have to find the one picture that isn't purr-fectly like the others.

©Karen Kuhlman

Puzzle 16: Among the Ruins

"I thought Mom said we were going to the mall!"

©Elizabeth Cárdenas-Nelson

A

B

C

D

E

1 2 3 4 5

Keep Track

9 Changes

Puzzle 17: Fall Family Portrait

Although fall can be frosty, memories warm the soul.

©Elizabeth Cárdenas-Nelson

Easy

A

B

C

D

E

1 2 3 4 5

Keep Track

9 Changes

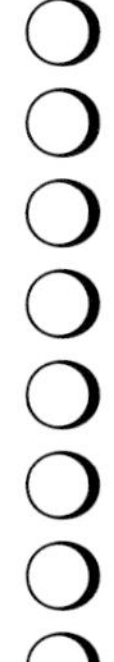

Puzzle 18: Say It with a Smile

These bright smiles can easily distract you from picking out all of the changes in this puzzle.

©Karen Kuhlman

Keep Track

9 Changes

A B C D E

1 2 3 4 5

Puzzle 19: Sweet Siblings

"I can't see my brother's hands — is he the one who keeps giving me bunny ears?"

Easy

A

B

C

D

E

1 2 3 4 5

Keep Track

9 Changes

Puzzle 20: Tourist Trap

"No, seriously — do my eyes look glassy?"

Easy

Keep Track

9 Changes

1 2 3 4 5

A B C D E

Puzzle 21: Clownin' Around

Watch out for the hall of mirrors in this circus of a puzzle!

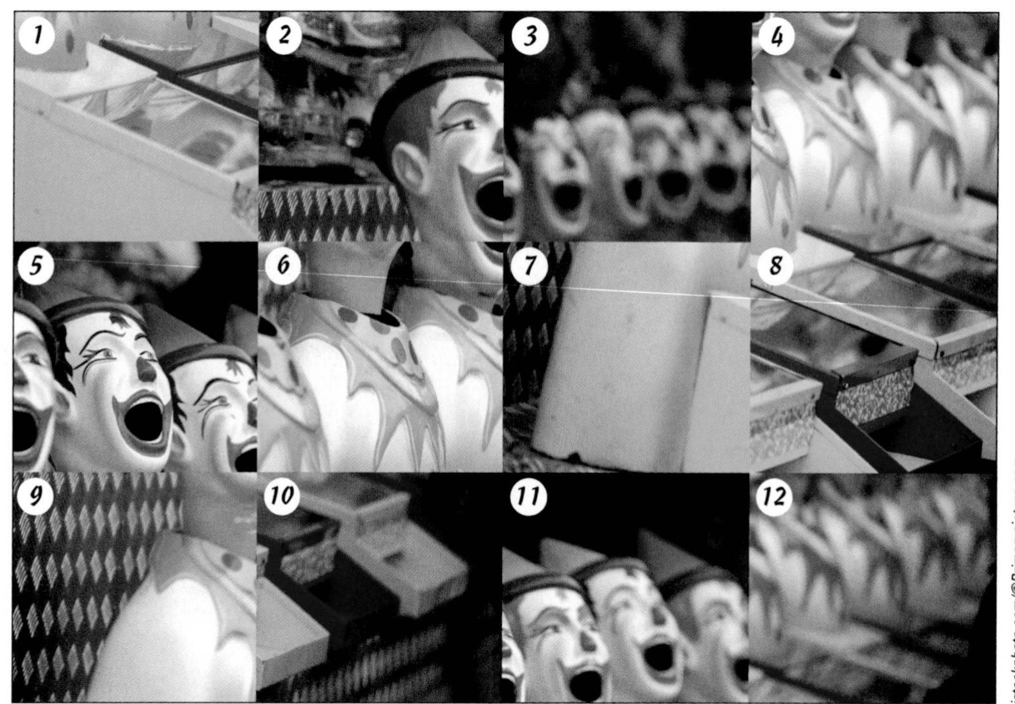

KEEP TRACK

Puzzle 22: Sail Away, Sail Away . . .

If you find your attention drifting while trying to spot the different picture in this puzzle, take a break on the deck and collect your concentration.

Puzzle 23: All about the Accessories

Girls *must* be born with an instinctual ability to accessorize.

A
B
C
D
E

1 2 3 4 5

Keep Track

8 Changes

○
○
○
○
○
○
○
○

Puzzle 24: Rustic Charm

Pots, pines, plants, and plenty of appeal . . . a great place to relax and explore.

Keep Track

8 Changes

Puzzle 25: Surf's Up!

See whether you can catch a break and find all the changes swimming in this sea of surfboards.

©istockphoto.com/Randolph Jay Braun

A

B

C

D

E

1 2 3 4 5

Keep Track

7 Changes

○ ○ ○ ○ ○ ○ ○

Puzzle 26: Heartfelt Sentiments

Sweet treats for the body and soul.

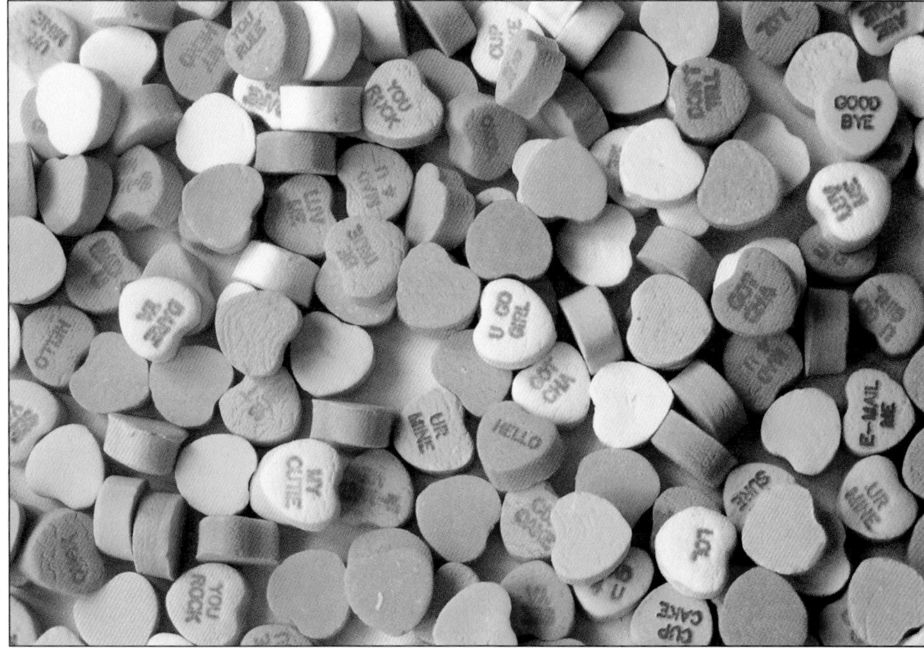

©Lindsay Lefevere

	1	2	3	4	5
A					
B					
C					
D					
E					

Easy

Keep Track

9 Changes

○ ○ ○ ○ ○ ○ ○ ○ ○

Puzzle 27: Dining Al Fresco in Mexico

This restaurant has a great concept to get diners to eat quickly . . . no seats!

Easy

Keep Track

11 Changes

○ ○ ○ ○ ○ ○ ○ ○ ○ ○ ○

1 2 3 4 5

A B C D E

Puzzle 28: Let Them Eat Cake!

Well, people probably *would* eat the cake if no one was afraid to cut such a picturesque piece of work.

Easy

A

B

C

D

E

1 2 3 4 5

Keep Track

8 Changes

Puzzle 29: Say What?

"Whaddaya mean there's no gifts under there for me?"

©Tracy Conlin

Easy

A

B

C

D

E

1 2 3 4 5

Keep Track

10 Changes

Puzzle 30: Fender Bender

Although it looks like a multicar pileup on the local interstate, it's actually the scene from under some child's bed.

©istockphoto.com/Anthony Marsh

Keep Track

9 Changes

A

B

C

D

E

1 2 3 4 5

Puzzle 31: Don't Blink!

Take a good, long look — it's going to take more than just whiskers and wit to figure out which cat is different from the others.

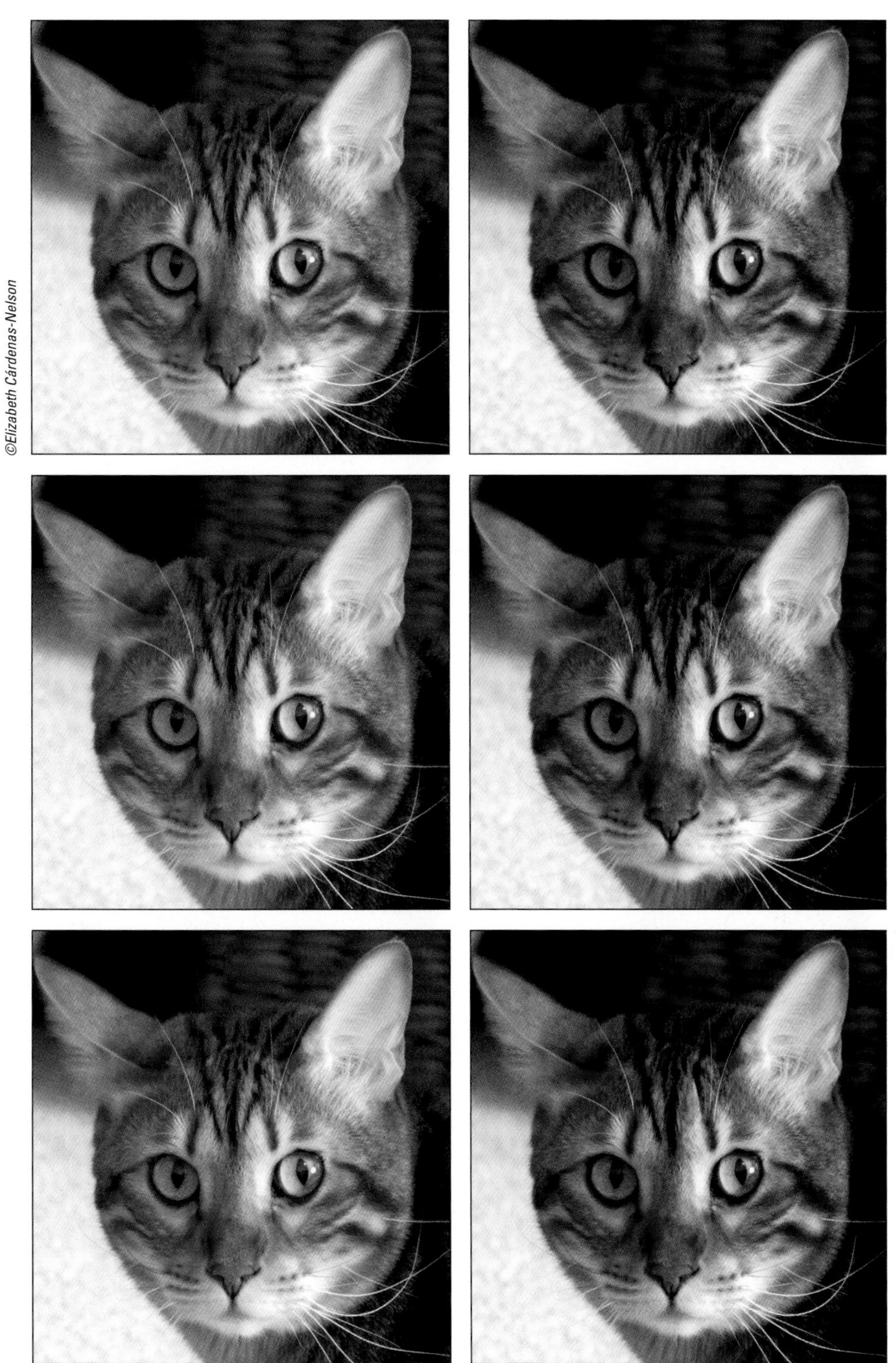

Puzzle 32: Bricks, Balconies, and Balusters

Built with Old World charm, this building can charm you out of noticing some of this puzzle's changes.

Tricky

A

B

C

D

E

1 2 3 4 5

Keep Track

9 Changes

○ ○ ○ ○ ○ ○ ○ ○ ○

Puzzle 33: Fully Equipped

Now only if he'd actually *use* the tools he painstakingly organized!

©istockphoto.com/Brian Sullivan

A
B
C
D
E

1 2 3 4 5

Keep Track

11 Changes

Puzzle 34: Putting the Kart before the Horsepower

"Forget that battery — I run on girl power!"

©Julie Conlin

A

B

C

D

E

1 2 3 4 5

Tricky

Keep Track

10 Changes

Puzzle 35: Breezy Palms

Although you won't find 29 palms — or 29 changes, for that matter — you'll find plenty here to keep you looking.

©Elizabeth Cárdenas-Nelson

Tricky

A

B

C

D

E

1 2 3 4 5

Keep Track

10 Changes

Puzzle 36: Around and Around We Go

Caution: Putting this puzzle together may cause dizziness.

©David Nelson

KEEP TRACK

Puzzle 37: Work It, Girl!

"I am *so* fierce! I can't decide whether to try out for Cirque du Soleil or America's Next Top Model!"

©Jennifer Connolly

Puzzle 38: Totems at Attention

Don't get too dizzy with the details that you miss the changes hidden here.

©istockphoto.com/Kenneth Cheung

A B C D E

1 2 3 4 5

Tricky

Keep Track

10 Changes

Puzzle 39: Suburban Serenity

Perfect neighborhood, perfect house, and a picket fence to boot.

©istockphoto.com/Michael Shake

A B C D E

1 2 3 4 5

Tricky

Keep Track

10 Changes

Puzzle 40: Wings of Change

These breezy butterflies are bursting with changes.

Tricky

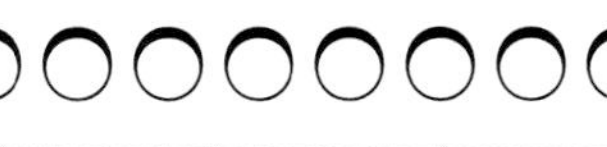

1 2 3 4 5

A B C D E

Puzzle 41: Jolly Trolley Time

You just can't beat taking the trolley to the bay on a beautiful day in San Francisco.

©Kevin Kirschner

Tricky

A
B
C
D
E

1 2 3 4 5

Keep Track

12 Changes

Puzzle 42: A Classic Castle

For sale: Picture-perfect castle, complete with moat, wooded surroundings, and friendly, neighborhood fire-breathing dragon. Motivated seller!

©istockphoto.com/Michael Boubin

Tricky

A

B

C

D

E

1 2 3 4 5

Keep Track

10 Changes

Puzzle 43: Food and Flora

If you stop to smell the flowers, you might miss your lunch reservation!

©Elizabeth Cárdenas-Nelson

A
B
C
D
E

1 2 3 4 5

Keep Track

12 Changes

○ ○ ○ ○ ○ ○ ○ ○ ○ ○ ○ ○

Puzzle 44: Horsin' Around with the Family

To catch all the changes this puzzle contains, you have to rein in your concentration and bridle distractions.

Tricky

Keep Track

14 Changes

○
○
○
○
○
○
○
○
○
○
○
○
○
○

Puzzle 45: Climbing Higher

"The thin air must be getting to me . . . I think I just saw a cow floating around!"

istockphoto.com/©Jacom Stephens

Tricky

A

B

C

D

E

1 2 3 4 5

Keep Track

7 Changes

Tricky

Puzzle 46: Junk in the Trunk

You can find lots of places to spot changes in this puzzle, especially considering all the trunk space.

©Elizabeth Cárdenas-Nelson

A B C D E

1 2 3 4 5

Keep Track

11 Changes

Puzzle 47: Don't Be a Pansy

Although this puzzle is tricky, don't wilt under the pressure of putting it together.

KEEP TRACK

Puzzle 48: Tie One On

Don't get tied into knots trying to wrap your head around the changes in this puzzle.

©Lindsay Lefevere

A B C D E

1 2 3 4 5

Keep Track

10 Changes

○ ○ ○ ○ ○ ○ ○ ○ ○ ○

Puzzle 49: Trackside Traveler

The only thing worse than missing the bus is missing the train.

©Elizabeth Cárdenas-Nelson

A

B

C

D

E

1 2 3 4 5

Tricky

Keep Track

9 Changes

Puzzle 50: Airspeed, Altitude, Altimeter, Oh My!

Although you may not be able to read all the gauges, you just need to be able to spot all the changes.

©istockphoto.com/Lucian

A B C D E

1 2 3 4 5

Keep Track

10 Changes

Puzzle 51: A Book Lover's Retreat

Custom-made bookshelves: $20,000. Rare, first editions bought on an Internet auction site: $70,000. Getting someone to actually dust the books and bookshelves: Priceless.

A B C D E

1 2 3 4 5

Tricky

Keep Track

10 Changes

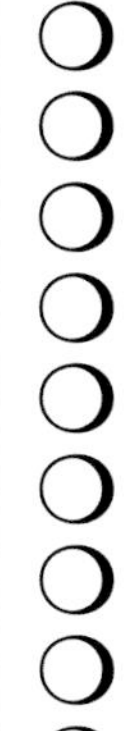

Puzzle 52: Cozying Up to the Canal

Take in all the sights — and changes — while your eyes stroll along the canal.

Keep Track

9 Changes

Tricky

Puzzle 53: Backyard Barbecue

Nothing says home like a barbecue on the patio — you can smell it cookin' from here!

©Doris Nelson

A

B

C

D

E

1 2 3 4 5

Keep Track

8 Changes

Puzzle 54: Welcome Home

Even under threatening skies, a brightly painted visitor's center sends a warm welcome.

A B C D E

1 2 3 4 5

Keep Track

10 Changes

Puzzle 55: Flower Power

You may not be thinking, "Peace!" until you discover the one picture that's different.

Puzzle 56: Just Lion Around

Take some pride in your puzzling abilities and get this lion put together licketysplit.

KEEP TRACK

Tricky

Puzzle 57: Lots o' Luggage

Look closely enough, and you may find all the changes in this puzzle — as well as the luggage you lost on your last flight.

Tricky

Keep Track

9 Changes

1 2 3 4 5

A B C D E

Puzzle 58: Chomping at the Bit

Kids and kittens — they always like the wrapping and ribbons better than the actual gifts!

©Karen Kuhlman

Tricky

A

B

C

D

E

1 2 3 4 5

Keep Track

9 Changes

○
○
○
○
○
○
○
○
○

Puzzle 59: Pole Position

That's one souvenir that definitely *won't* fit into the overhead luggage bin.

A

B

C

D

E

1 2 3 4 5

Keep Track

11 Changes

Tricky

Puzzle 60: A Grand Vista

Don't look down!

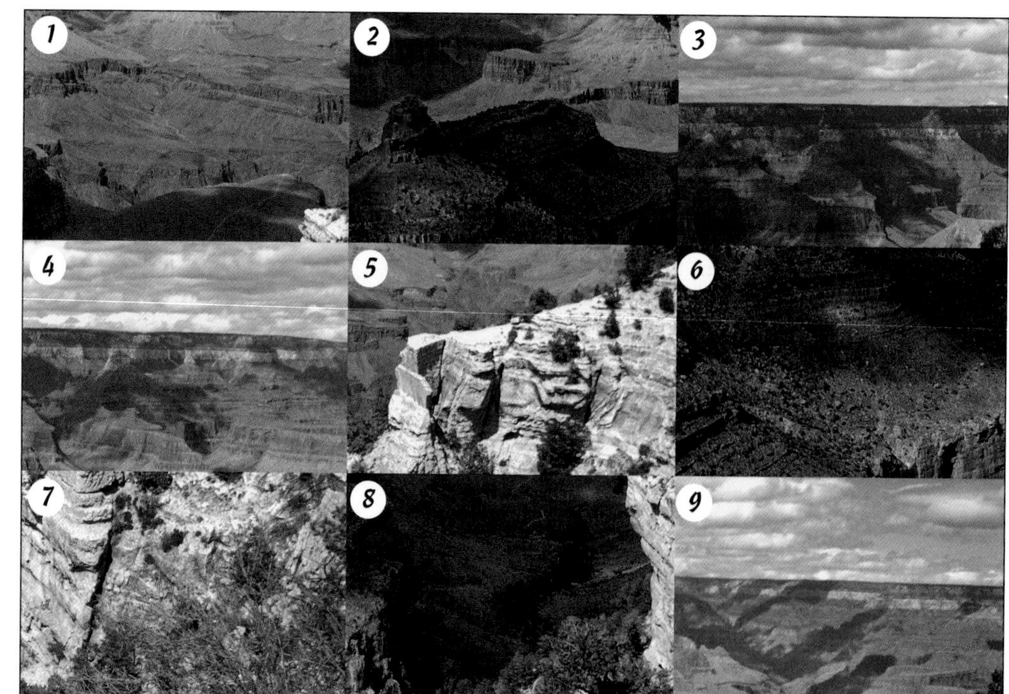

Puzzle 61: Grins and Giggles

Okay, so you may be forming more of a grimace than a grin, but give yourself some time, and you'll figure out which one of these is different.

©Kevin Kirschner

Puzzle 62: Brick by Brick

If you can't find all the changes, you may be left feeling a few bricks shy . . .

Tough

A
B
C
D
E

1 2 3 4 5

Keep Track

8 Changes

Tough

Puzzle 63: Artful Renovation

"Well, the real estate agent said that we needed to take down the personal photos and add some art. I thought this might jazz up the entryway for potential buyers."

©istockphoto.com/Kent Weakley

Keep Track

10 Changes

A

B

C

D

E

1 2 3 4 5

Puzzle 64: What's Good for the Goose . . .

Wild Kingdom for toddlers . . .

©Joan Taylor

A B C D E

1 2 3 4 5

Tough

Keep Track

9 Changes

Puzzle 65: Getting a Great View

If you want a room with a balcony on this street, you're in luck!

©Elizabeth Cárdenas-Nelson

Keep Track

10 Changes

Puzzle 66: Free Fallin'

Jump in and take a stab at finding all the changes in this puzzle.

©David Nelson

A
B
C
D
E

1 2 3 4 5

Keep Track

11 Changes

Puzzle 67: Don't Miss the Boat

Even if you miss the boat, don't miss the changes in this puzzle, or you'll be sunk.

©Kathy Kuhlman

A
B
C
D
E

1 2 3 4 5

Tough

Keep Track

8 Changes

○ ○ ○ ○ ○ ○ ○ ○

Puzzle 68: Reaching New Heights

Buckle down if you plan to get a foothold on all the changes contained in this puzzle.

©Jennifer Connolly

A

B

C

D

E

1 2 3 4 5

Tough

Keep Track

11 Changes

Puzzle 69: Flowers and Foliage

See whether you can get this puzzle put together without wilting.

KEEP TRACK

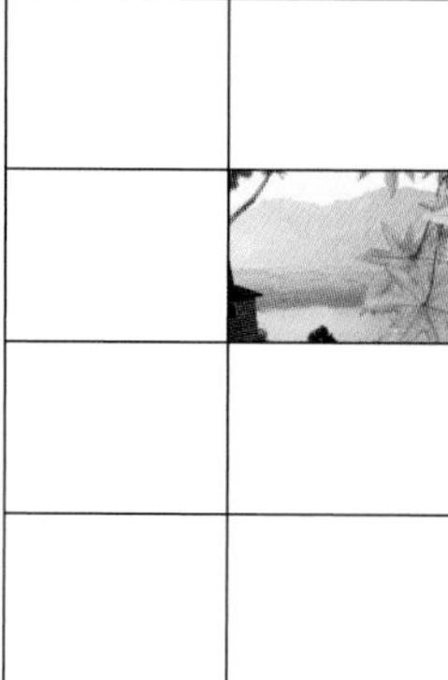

Puzzle 70: Dive On In!

Taking the plunge never looked so inviting!

KEEP TRACK

Puzzle 71: Where Are the Pink Flamingoes?

These birds may fool you into thinking that they're flamingoes, but don't be easily fooled into missing any changes in this puzzle.

©Elizabeth Cárdenas-Nelson

	1	2	3	4	5
A					
B					
C					
D					
E					

Keep Track

9 Changes

Tough

Puzzle 72: Down in the Valley

You can see for miles, but can you see all of the changes hidden here?

A B C D E

1 2 3 4 5

Keep Track

9 Changes

Puzzle 73: Full of Hot Air

Fire up your brain power and put this balloon together so that it's ready for take off.

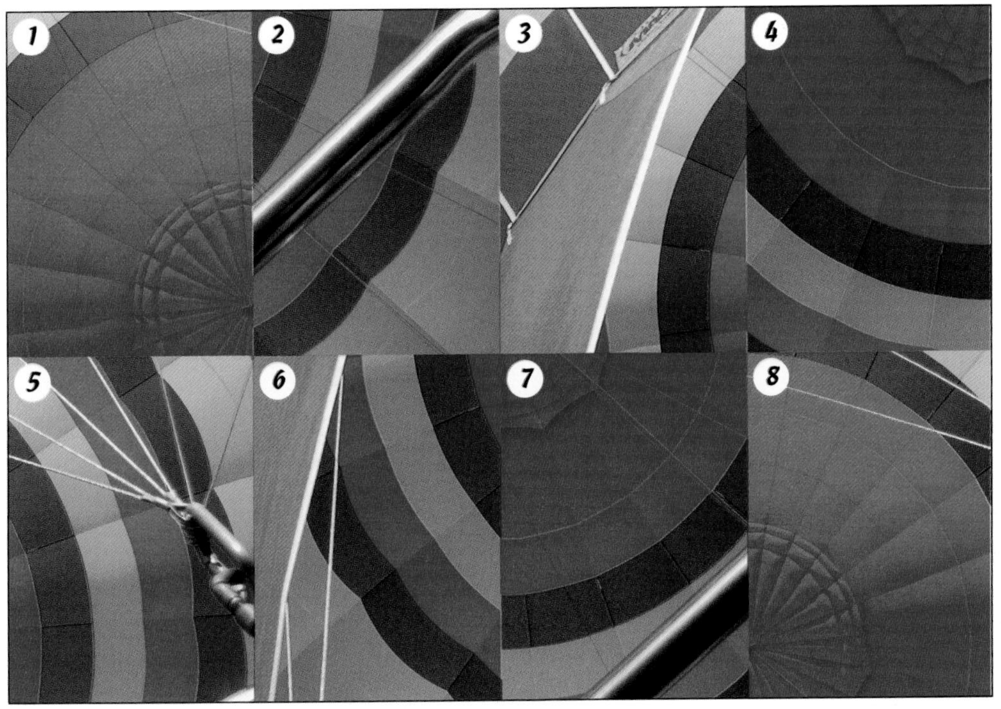

KEEP TRACK

Tough

Puzzle 74: On the Hunt

"Now where'd I put that remote? I'm telling you, I'd lose my pacifier if it weren't buttoned to me!"

istockphoto.com/©Zsolt Nyulaszi

A B C D E

1 2 3 4 5

Keep Track

12 Changes

Puzzle 75: Read All About It Al Fresco

A cold drink and a little fresh air may help you find all the changes at this café.

A

B

C

D

E

1 2 3 4 5

Tough

Keep Track

10 Changes

Puzzle 76: Make It Work — STAT!

"Hang on, guys . . . give me a minute . . . I can't get a cell signal out here to call my wife and let her know I'll be late!"

A B C D E

1 2 3 4 5

Keep Track

10 Changes

○ ○ ○ ○ ○ ○ ○ ○ ○ ○

Puzzle 77: Architecture with Inspiration

Even an office park can give a facelift to the community when it's inspired by Frank Lloyd Wright.

A

B

C

D

E

1 2 3 4 5

Tough

Keep Track

10 Changes

Puzzle 78: All Revved Up

You don't have to be a mechanic to figure out what's different in one of these pictures.

©Carmen Krikorian

Puzzle 79: Living on the Edge

One wrong move piecing together this puzzle, and you may be over a barrel.

KEEP TRACK

Puzzle 80: A Colorful Cavalcade of Containers

Don't get lost searching for changes in this plastic paradise.

©Kevin Kirschner

Diabolical

Keep Track

9 Changes

Puzzle 81: Peering over Navy Pier

This waterfront scene harbors a hefty amount of changes that will leave you spinning.

Diabolical

Keep Track

14 Changes

○○○○○○○○○○○○○○

Puzzle 82: If Walls Could Talk

Stepping too far to the left on that ledge may put you on your back, but it will land you a great picture!

©Carmen Krikorian

Keep Track

9 Changes

5 4 3 2 1

E D C B A

Diabolical

Puzzle 83: No Horsin' Around

You can really earn your stripes if you can get this puzzle put together.

©Elizabeth Cárdenas-Nelson

KEEP TRACK

Puzzle 84: Angles and Architecture

Time to get out your T-square and transform these pieces into an actual picture.

KEEP TRACK

Puzzle 85: Sticks and Stones . . .

Spotting changes here will put you between a rock and a hard place.

Keep Track

8 Changes

Puzzle 86: Up, Up, and Away!

Leap tall buildings in a single bound . . . spot all changes in a single sitting!

©Sara Kuhlman

A

B

C

D

E

1 2 3 4 5

Keep Track

14 Changes

Puzzle 87: A Colorful Carnival Landscape

Exactly how many times do we have to ride to the top of this Ferris wheel to find the elephant ear stand?

Diabolical

Keep Track

9 Changes

1 2 3 4 5

A B C D E

Puzzle 88: Mmm, Mmm, Good!

If you're not careful figuring out which picture is different from the others, you're gonna get licked!

Puzzle 89: Speed Trap

Proof that you weren't actually speeding — although taking a picture while driving may be considered reckless driving. . . .

Puzzle 90: One Man's Trash . . .

You can find a treasure trove of changes within this wannabe garage sale.

©Kevin Kirschner

A B C D E

1 2 3 4 5

Keep Track

10 Changes

○ ○ ○ ○ ○ ○ ○ ○ ○ ○

Puzzle 91: A Room with a View

Enjoy the view, overlooking the harbor, but don't overlook any changes in this puzzle.

©Elizabeth Cárdenas-Nelson

A

B

C

D

E

1 2 3 4 5

Keep Track

11 Changes

Puzzle 92: Views from the Valley

This place is perfect with valley vistas for miles!

Keep Track

10 Changes

5 4 3 2 1

E D C B A

Puzzle 93: Botanical Beauties

Stopping to smell the flowers means you're likely to miss the changes amongst these bewildering botanicals.

Bewildering

Keep Track

9 Changes

A B C D E

1 2 3 4 5

Puzzle 94: Switches in the Swatches

Pick through these patterns and iron out any changes you see between the two pictures.

©Elizabeth Cárdenas-Nelson

A

B

C

D

E

1 2 3 4 5

Keep Track

9 Changes

○ ○ ○ ○ ○ ○ ○ ○ ○

Puzzle 95: Mountain Town

Unbeknownst to this small town, Area 51 has been operating on the other side of that mountain for years.

©Carmen Krikorian

A

B

C

D

E

1 2 3 4 5

Keep Track

10 Changes

Puzzle 96: Three Fair Maidens

How well can you fare spotting changes at this fair?

Keep Track

9 Changes

○○○○○○○○○

1 2 3 4 5

A B C D E

Puzzle 97: Kooky, Spooky Castle

"Hurry and snap the picture — it *was* Cousin It that I saw in the upstairs window!"

©Elizabeth Cárdenas-Nelson

A

B

C

D

E

1 2 3 4 5

Keep Track

9 Changes

Puzzle 98: Hills and High Places

Harbor views and valley vistas make this landscape a lush escape.

A B C D E

1 2 3 4 5

Keep Track

10 Changes

Puzzle 99: Purr-fectly Poised

These statuesque cats are playing innocent when it comes to the changes lurking throughout this puzzle.

© Weems Smith Hutto

A

B

C

D

E

1 2 3 4 5

Keep Track

10 Changes

Puzzle 100: Neighborhood Watch

Why is it that the realtor's pictures are never as clear as they should be?

KEEP TRACK

Part III
Checking Your Work — No Peeking!

"Yes, I get it! You're solving puzzles at the 'Master' level."

In this part . . .

Stop! Do not pass GO! Do not collect $200!

We mean it. Think about it before you flip open this part. Do you really want to see the solution before you've completely solved the puzzle? You're only cheating yourself if you check out the solutions contained in this part before you solve the puzzles. Picture puzzles take more than sharp attention to detail and vast concentration — they also take a bit of self-control. So restrain yourself. Keep your fingers from flipping to the pages in this part until you're good and ready.

Puzzle 1: Easy, Breezy, Beautiful

1	4
2	3

Puzzle 2: Buyer Beware!

A2: Purple stripe changed to blue. **A2:** Tag removed on top of hat. **B1:** Yellow stripe on brim changed purple. **B2:** Glasses changed to sunglasses. **B4:** Tag removed from brim. **B4:** Watch face added. **C2 and C3:** Collar changed to white. **D2:** White stripe changed to blue. **D4:** Emblem added to shirt.

Puzzle 3: Slip into Something Comfortable!

A3: Design changed on pink slipper. **A4:** Black diamond missing. **A5:** Orange diamonds changed to black. **B2:** Blue diamond missing. **C1:** Slipper color changed from pink to green. **C4:** Blue slipper changed to green. **D2:** Diamonds made larger. **E5:** Slipper changed color from orange to white.

Puzzle 4: Home on the Range

B2: Line of shrubs shorter. **B2:** Tree shortened. **C1:** Animals removed. **C2:** Animal laying down removed. **C4:** Animal added. **D1:** Animal added. **E3:** Branch on ground removed. **E5:** Tree stump added.

Puzzle 5: A Trendy Spot for a Trim

B2: Hair dryer added. **B3:** Bottle color changed to blue. **B3:** Black bottle added. **C2:** Magazine added to chair. **C4:** White box added to wall. **C5:** Drawer handle removed. **E5:** Wire table added.

Puzzle 6: Con-grad-ulations!

A5: Red balloon removed. **C2:** Man's shirt color changed from blue to green. **C5:** Purse changed color from brown to lavender. **D2:** Red tulip added. **D3:** School crest removed from diploma. **C5, D5, and E5:** Tulips added. **E2:** Green leaf enlarged, covering small yellow tulip.

Puzzle 7: Kickin' Back on the Beach

C1: Missing drink from chair's cup holder. **C4:** Missing hat. **C4:** Blue shape on towel changed to purple. **C4:** Removed chair's footrest. **D1:** Yellow color on kickboard changed to red. **D3:** Missing one stripe from chair. **D5:** Missing one stripe from chair.

Puzzle 8: Here Kitty, Kitty!

6	5
4	1
3	2

Puzzle 9: Undercover Café!

A3: Top missing on building. **A3:** Line missing on roof. **B4:** Sign made larger. **B4:** Railing made shorter. **C2:** Color changed from purple to blue on umbrella. **C5:** Post added on stairs. **D2:** Top of umbrella changed from white to black. **D3:** Black bag made larger. **D3:** Part of manhole missing. **D4:** White swirl missing on umbrella. **E5:** Design on chair missing.

Puzzle 10: Wrap It Up!

B1: Pink string removed. **B4:** Pink ribbon added. **C1:** Flower changed from pink to blue. **C2:** Yellow flower added. **C5:** Wrapping paper square changed color from blue to yellow. **D4:** Crochet ribbon added to flowers. **E3:** Leaves added. **E4:** Leaves removed.

Puzzle 11: Float Like a Butterfly

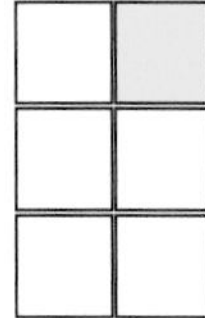

Missing a flower bud.

Puzzle 12: Hats off to the Ladies!

A1: Balloons added. **A1:** Eyes closed. **A2:** Orange cone added. **A4:** White tent added. **B4:** Oval logo added to jacket. **C3:** Silver bolts removed from blue on cart. **D4:** Extra bolt added. **D5:** Number 32 sign changed colors. **E2:** Powersports logo removed. **E3:** Wheel enlarged. **E4:** Rims changed color from tan to purple.

Puzzle 13: Oil Can!

A2: Purple flower added to straw hat. **A4:** Flag with red cross added. **B2:** Blue scarf changed to green. **B4:** Holes added to straw hat. **B4:** Letters reversed. **B5:** Lock on door moved. **C2:** Gray shirt made longer. **C3:** Colors reversed on dogs eyes. **D4:** Extra wheel added to lawn mower. **E5:** Dog bowl moved.

Puzzle 14: A Royal Pair

B1 and B2: Flowers in pot changed color from pink to white. **B2:** Earring color changed to blue. **C4:** Missing ear. **D2:** Bracelet changed from pink to purple. **D3:** Character on button changed to blue flower. **D5:** Second ruffled removed from shoulder of dress. **E4:** Missing blue flower on brush. **E5:** Missing pink beads.

Puzzle 15: Furry Valentine

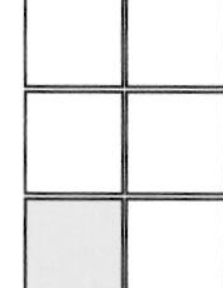

Flower added to box.

Puzzle 16: Among the Ruins

C1: Pennants removed. **C4:** Concrete made larger. **C5:** Concrete design made larger. **D2:** Vase added. **D3:** Bicycle color changed from blue to green. **D3:** Girls' top color changed from blue to pink. **D3:** Sign added on wall. **D3:** Girls' pants color changed from blue to tan. **D4:** Brick on wall removed.

Puzzle 17: Fall Family Portrait

A2: Glasses changed to sunglasses. **A3:** Part of corn husks removed. **C4:** Sleeve on lady made longer. **C5:** Pumpkin added. **D2:** Tag on wheelchair color changed from silver to black. **D5:** Pumpkin made larger in basket. **D5:** Pumpkins made larger. **E1:** Cap on wheel made larger. **E4:** Man's socks color changed from tan to blue.

Puzzle 18: Say It with a Smile

A2: Word OF removed from sign. **A3:** Sunburst made larger. **B2:** Hair removed from forehead. **C4:** Lipstick added. **C5:** Strap removed from shirt. **D3:** Tie changed color. **D5:** Design removed from shirt. **E1:** Letter C removed from nameplate. **E1:** Black bar on desk smaller.

Puzzle 19: Sweet Siblings

A3: Leaves added. **B3:** Ear removed from girl's hat. **C1:** Board changed color. **C2:** "Go team" added to shirt. **C3:** Flower added to girl's sweatshirt. **C4:** Strap removed from glove. **C5:** Board made smaller. **D1:** Band on sweatshirt changed from light gray to dark gray. **E5:** Wheel bearing made larger.

Puzzle 20: Tourist Trap

A1: Extra piece of wood added. **B3:** Eyeballs changed to black color. **B5:** Extra clear glasses added. **C2:** Extra mug added. **C3:** Wrist watch color changed from brown to blue. **C3:** Necklace removed. **D5:** Design on mug changed. **E1:** Extra box stacked. **E2:** Color of purse changed from tan to green.

Puzzle 21: Clownin' Around

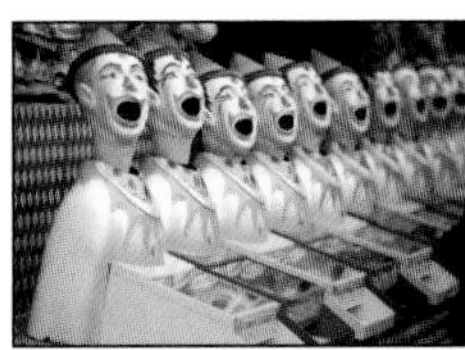

2	5	11	3
9	6	4	12
7	1	8	10

Puzzle 22: Sail Away, Sail Away . . .

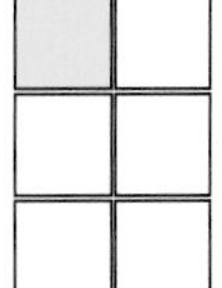

Blue triangle on sail is changed to purple.

Puzzle 23: All about the Accessories

A4: Shades on sunglasses changed color. **B5:** Bell missing on handlebars. **C3:** Bow added to purse. **C4:** Flower design added to shirt. **D1:** Rear wheel made smaller. **D5:** Screw missing from front forks on bike. **E1:** Peddle added to rear wheel. **E4:** Shoe changed color from pink to blue.

Puzzle 24: Rustic Charm

B3: Window removed. **C2:** Wood braces changed color to red. **C3:** Wood beam made solid. **C3:** Wood brace removed. **D2:** Sign removed from window. **D4:** Barrel planter made taller. **D5:** Blue planter removed. **E5:** Blue planter added.

Puzzle 25: Surf's Up!

A4: Surfboard missing. **B1:** Brown stripe missing on surfboard. **C1:** Line made larger on surfboard. **C4:** Blue arrow made smaller. **D1:** Footprint changed color from purple to green. **E1:** Plant added. **E5:** Leaf made larger.

Puzzle 26: Heartfelt Sentiments

A3: "You" added to heart. **A5:** Button added. **B4:** Orange heat changed color to pink. **C1:** Pink circle added. **C4:** Purple heart changed color to blue. **D2:** White heart added. **D3:** Blue heart added. **D3:** "Hello" removed from heart. **E4:** "Girl" added to heart.

Puzzle 27: Dining Al Fresco in Mexico

A3: Green butterfly added. **A3:** Circle flower pattern made bigger. **B2:** Umbrella changed color from white to red. **B5:** Pattern on tree added. **C1:** Yellow flowers added. **C2:** Statue's pant's changed to green color. **C3:** Drink added. **C3:** Red color added to fabric. **C4:** Item on table changed color from white to red. **D1:** Part of wheel removed. **E3:** Bottom of stand removed.

Puzzle 28: Let Them Eat Cake!

A2: Spout changed color from gold to green. **B4:** Red rose added. **C2:** Daisy added. **C3:** Yellow rose added. **C5:** Silver candle made taller. **D2:** Butterfly added. **E2:** Bird missing. **E5:** Ball on handle changed to red.

Puzzle 29: Say What?

A3: Ornament changed color. **B5:** Teddy bear ornament added. **C1:** Angel added. **C3:** Handkerchief added on dog. **C5:** Apple ornament removed. **D1:** Wrapping paper changed color from blue to orange. **D1:** Penguin removed from wrapping paper. **D4:** Stuffed mole added. **E4:** Snowman on wrapping paper is reversed. **E5:** Wrapping bow moved and made larger.

Puzzle 30: Fender Bender

A5: Car bottom changed from gray to green. **B1:** Headlight missing. **B5:** Windshield made larger. **C1:** White grill added. **C3:** Logo missing on car grill. **C3:** License plate changed numbers. **D1:** Front changed from red to blue. **D4:** Red color missing from front of truck. **E2:** Headlight made larger.

Puzzle 31: Don't Blink!

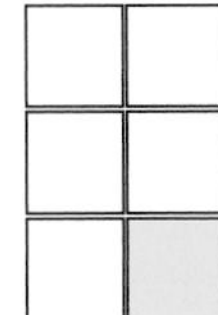

Stripe near eye removed.

Puzzle 32: Bricks, Balconies, and Balusters

A3: Window panes changed. **B5:** Window added. **B5:** Decorative circles over red awning have thinner outer circles. **C3:** Topiary added to left side of balcony doorway. **C3:** Red flowers removed from bouquet on right side of balcony doorway. **C5:** Cement finial removed from balcony. **D1:** Small white box removed from side of building. **D2:** Decorative cement element lengthened. **D3:** Shade changed color.

Puzzle 33: Fully Equipped

A2: Wrench made smaller. **A3:** Bottle added. **A3:** Screwdriver added. **A4:** Yellow jar made larger. **B4:** String missing. **C1:** Thermometer turned upside down. **C1:** Tape changed from blue to green. **C5:** Outlet missing. **D1:** Black object added to wall. **D3:** Screwdriver missing. **D5:** Extra metal added to pegboard.

Puzzle 34: Putting the Kart before the Horsepower

A4: Pole removed. **B4:** Tire added. **C2:** Watch replaced with bracelet. **C3:** Part on cart changed color from red to blue. **C3:** Blue on jacket removed. **C4:** Purple on cart changed to red. **C5:** Blue container added. **D2:** Red bar removed from front of battery. **D4:** Gold on wheel arm made larger. **E2:** "W" missing from "www".

Puzzle 35: Breezy Palms

B5: Light bulb color changed. **C2:** Light bulb color changed. **C3:** Silver finial missing. **D2:** White speaker added. **D5:** Rope added to post. **D5:** Shadow/color of wood changed. **E1:** Missing white ring on tree. **E2:** Missing light. **E3:** Light bulb added. **E4:** Orange design added to flag.

Puzzle 36: Around and Around We Go

9	8	5
2	1	6
3	7	4

Puzzle 37: Work It, Girl!

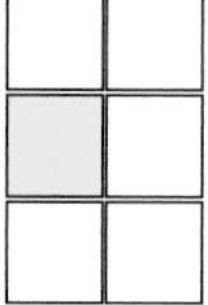

White dots missing under eye on right side of her nose.

Puzzle 38: Totems at Attention

A4: Red color on head changed to green. **A4:** Eye changed from circular to crescent shape. **B2:** Orange shape added to head. **B5:** Black-and-white design on wing changed to green and white. **C3:** Feather missing. **C4:** Black-red-and-white design made larger. **D1:** Missing part of arm. **D2:** Two white dots changed orange. **D2:** Top wave design changed. **D5:** Oval changed to square.

Puzzle 39: Suburban Serenity

B2: Shade missing from window. **C2:** Circle window covered. **C3:** Window grid missing. **C4:** Row of windows missing. **D2:** Plant made larger. **D2:** Finial missing from fencepost. **D3:** Window missing grid. **D3:** Column missing from porch. **D3:** Light made larger. **D4:** Post added.

Puzzle 40: Wings of Change

A2 and A3: Color on wings changed from red to green. **B2:** Color on wings changed from orange to blue. **B3:** Both strings made shorter. **B4:** Color on wing changed from blue to orange. **C1 and D2:** White changed to green. **C2:** Two green spaces combined on wing. **C3:** Pattern on wing changed. **C5:** Tip of wing removed. **D1:** Green added to tip of wing. **E2:** String added.

Puzzle 41: Jolly Trolley Time

A3: Buildings removed. **B1:** Flag missing. **B3:** Window missing on building. **C3:** Red car changed color to orange. **C5:** "B" missing from street sign. **D1** and **D2:** Windows reversed on trolley. **D2:** Item missing on trolley. **D3:** Gray car added. **D5:** Electrical box made taller. **E1:** Word on sign changed from "and" to "or". **E2:** Number "4" changed to number "5" on trolley. **E2:** Light on trolley changed from clear to green.

Puzzle 42: A Classic Castle

A3: Top of roof removed. **B1:** Tree made taller. **B1:** Window removed. **B2:** Roof changed color from blue to pink. **B3:** Window added. **B3:** Battlements combined. **C2:** Wall made longer. **C3:** Bridge made thicker. **D1:** Red design missing. **D2:** Window added.

Puzzle 43: Food and Flora

A3: Light added. **A4:** Exit sign added. **B3:** Flowers added. **B3:** Wood changed color from brown to green. **B4:** Wood beam removed. **C2:** Design on shutter removed. **C3:** Bear design added to wall. **C3:** Design on shutter changed to a heart. **C3:** Bear drawing added above window. **E1:** Purple flowers changed to red. **E2:** Yellow flower removed. **E5:** "Is" on sign changed to "in".

Puzzle 44: Horsin' Around with the Family

B3: WINTER is spelled WINTRE on orange shirt. **B3:** Blue lowercase "o" is filled in on orange shirt. **C1:** Button missing from button-down collar. **C2:** Horse's eye is larger. **C2:** Buckle added to bridle. **C3:** Strands of hair falling in girl's face removed. **C4:** Emblem added to collar of white turtleneck. **C5:** Flowers added to toddler's top. **D4:** Button removed from woman's jacket. **D4:** Button added to pocket of woman's jacket. **D5:** Zipper pull from man's jacket removed. **E1:** Button added to shirt. **E2:** Blue rope removed. **E5:** Part of design missing from toddler's pants.

Puzzle 45: Climbing Higher

A2: Hot air balloon added. **B2:** Colors reversed on balloon. **B4:** Red design on balloon changed to blue. **C3:** Balloon removed. **D5:** Balloon enlarged. **E2:** Basket removed from balloon. **E4:** Flag removed from balloon.

Puzzle 46: Junk in the Trunk

A1: Treetop added. **B5:** Elephant added. **C2:** Fence post removed. **C3:** Elephant removed. **C4:** Tusk removed. **C4:** Tusk longer. **C5:** Tail removed. **D3:** Tusk removed. **D3:** Plant added. **D5:** Turtle added. **E1:** Duck added.

Puzzle 47: Don't Be a Pansy

5	2	3
1	4	6

Puzzle 48: Tie One On

A3: Flower added to pattern on ribbon. **A4:** Pattern on ribbon changed from circle to square. **A5:** Extra stripes added to pattern on ribbon. **A5:** Paw print removed from ribbon. **B5:** Light-pink polka dots added to ribbon. **B5:** Brown ribbon with white dots replaced small spool of white ribbon with rabbit pattern. **C1:** Symbol removed from ribbon spool. **C3 and D2:** Pink daisy ribbon changed to yellow. **E2:** Blue gingham ribbon changed to purple. **E5:** White stripe in ribbon made smaller.

Puzzle 49: Trackside Traveler

C2: Bricks changed. **C5:** Box added to post. **D1:** Box color changed from white to pink. **D2:** Flowers added. **D3:** Orange circle removed. **D4:** Sign with "X" changed color from white to red. **D4:** Bar on post made lower. **E1:** Shirt color changed from gray to blue. **E2:** Concrete on post made higher.

Puzzle 50: Airspeed, Altitude, Altimeter, Oh My!

A2: Light changed color to orange. **A2:** Letter L removed. **B2:** Needle made longer and turned white. **B5:** Screw changed to knob. **C1:** Knob turned upside down. **D2:** Numeral "2" changed to "3". **D4:** Knob made larger. **E1:** Black label added. **E3:** Green arrow added. **E5:** UP changed to DOWN.

Puzzle 51: A Book Lover's Retreat

A1: Diamond design missing. **A1:** Ceiling piece added. **A3:** Design on top of bookshelf changed. **B2:** Sconce removed. **B4:** Book missing made larger. **D1:** Picture frame made larger. **D3:** Design on column made larger. **D5:** Books changed size and number. **E1:** Leaf added. **E4:** Book turned upside down.

Puzzle 52: Cozying Up to the Canal

B1: Window pane added. **C4:** Design added above windows. **C5:** Window pane removed. **D4:** Color added to building. **D5:** Light post added. **D5:** Half of post from railing removed. **E1:** Steel plate made larger. **E3:** Light removed. **E4:** Bolts removed.

Puzzle 53: Backyard Barbecue

A2: Umbrella changed color from gray to brown. **A4:** Large shrub added. **B2:** Painting made larger. **C3**: Yellow cup added. **C4:** Design on shirt removed. **C4:** Red bowl made larger. **D2:** Shorts changed color from blue to brown. **E5:** Legs missing from chair.

Puzzle 54: Welcome Home

A3: White chimney removed. **B2:** Window added. **B3:** Blue siding changed to roof shingles. **C4:** Roof changed color from green to brown. **D2:** Words reversed on sign. **D4:** Planter added. **D4:** Shrub made taller. **D5:** Sign changed color from blue to white. **E3:** Shrub removed. **E3:** Flowers changed color.

Puzzle 55: Flower Power

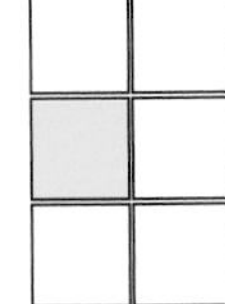

Another stigma added.

Puzzle 56: Just Lion Around

9	7	5
2	3	6
8	1	4

Puzzle 57: Lots o' Luggage

A2: Bag changed color from green to orange. **A3:** Metal circle added to bag. **A4:** Strap changed color from red to green. **C1:** Hard suitcase added. **C3:** Tag changed color from red to purple. **D1:** Tag made larger. **D5:** White stripe removed from bag. **D5:** Blue strap made larger. **E4:** Handle removed.

Puzzle 58: Chomping at the Bit

A1: Circle on wrapping paper changed color from green to pink. **C2:** Box on wrapping paper changed color from blue to orange. **C2:** "I" in "Birthday" is missing. **C3:** "A" is reversed **C4:** White stripe on cat is missing. **C4:** Cat's eyes changed color from green to blue. **D1:** Green design added to pink circle. **D3:** White icing on cupcake made larger. **E4:** Ribbon added.

Puzzle 59: Pole Position

B2: Window pane removed. **B4:** Eye on wing removed. **C1:** Wood log removed. **C3:** Feet changed color from yellow to dark red. **C3** and **C4:** Eyes changed color from gray to green. **D3:** Pane of window removed. **D4:** Writing on t-shirt removed. **E1:** Rock removed. **E4:** Letter "Y" on pants removed. **E4:** Different rock added.

Puzzle 60: A Grand Vista

3	4	9
2	1	5
6	8	7

Puzzle 61: Grins and Giggles

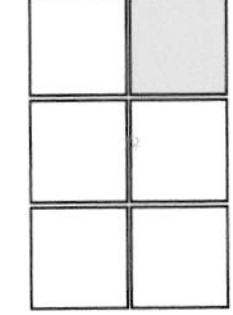

Missing white flower on shirt sleeve.

Puzzle 62: Brick by Brick

B1: Missing chimney. **B3:** Missing the words NATURAL HISTORY from the building. **B5:** Missing window air-conditioner. **C2:** Missing white bar in window. **D2:** Window air-conditioner added. **D3:** Part of sign missing. **E4:** Plant added in planter. **E5:** Fire hydrant different color.

Puzzle 63: Artful Renovation

A3: Background of star in circle changed to white. **B1:** Ceiling tile design enlarged. **B5:** Ceiling tile design flipped. **C3:** Robe changed from yellow to red. **C3:** Banner removed. **C4:** Man added. **D2:** Person added. **D3:** Sword lengthened. **E1:** Outer edge design changed to ceiling design. **E5:** Star added

Puzzle 64: What's Good for the Goose . . .

A3: Goose added. **C2:** Sleeve made longer. **C5:** Goose reversed. **D2:** Button changed color to pink. **E1:** Rock removed. **E2:** Sandal changed color from red to green. **E2:** Rock removed. **E3:** Flower added to sandal. **E5:** Rocks added.

Puzzle 65: Getting a Great View

A5: Colors reversed on restaurant sign. **B2:** Black spot removed from building. **B3:** Window removed. **B4:** Blinds removed from window. **D3:** Sign added. **D3:** Letters on Coke sign reversed. **E1:** Color of line changed from white to yellow. **E2:** Two pink awnings made into one. **E3:** Light post added. **E5:** Planter changed color to blue.

Puzzle 66: Free Fallin'

A2: Parachute color changed from blue to pink. **A4:** Missing part of parachute. **A5:** Yellow strap missing. **B4:** Glasses are shaded. **C3:** Shadow filled in. **C4:** Buckle added to strap. **C5:** Shoe laces changed to pink. **D3:** Goggles missing. **D3:** Color on leg changed. **D3:** Missing white label. **D5:** Shoe color changed.

Puzzle 67: Don't Miss the Boat

A4: Building shortened. **A5:** Red pole shortened. **C2:** Necklace removed. **C3:** Purple strap removed. **C5:** Window added. **D5:** Boat name changed. **E3:** White flower on dress changed to pink. **E5:** Bench removed from boat.

Puzzle 68: Reaching New Heights

A4: Cable padding shortened. **A5:** Foothold added. **B3:** Foothold moved lower. **B4:** Decal removed from helmet. **B5:** Knothole in wood changed shape. **C1:** Nails removed from top of wood. **C4:** Buckle from leg strap removed. **D2:** Knothole added. **D4:** Strap lengthened. **E1:** Foothold added. **E3:** Foothold changed color from yellow to red.

Puzzle 69: Flowers and Foliage

6	1
7	4
3	5
8	2

Puzzle 70: Dive On In!

6	12	8	3
1	4	7	9
11	2	5	10

Puzzle 71: Where Are the Pink Flamingoes?

A4: Ridge on roof removed. **B2:** Railing made longer. **B5:** Post made longer. **C1:** Rock made larger. **C2:** Cross railing is missing. **C5:** Fence made longer. **D4:** Bird removed. **E4:** Duck is moved. **E5:** Rock is missing.

Puzzle 72: Down in the Valley

C2: Building changed color from white to tan. **C2:** Windows made full. **C4:** Extra row of windows added to building. **D4:** Car changed color from blue to purple. **D4:** Blue garbage cans made larger. **D4:** Blue car added. **D5:** Two window panes removed from window. **E2:** Palm tree added. **E5:** Part of window missing.

Puzzle 73: Full of Hot Air

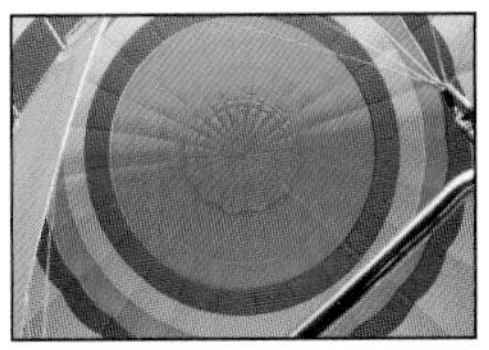

3	1	8	5
6	4	7	2

Puzzle 74: On the Hunt

A1: Bee removed. **A3:** Butterfly changed from purple to orange. **A4:** Eyeballs removed from alligator. **A5:** Bee added. **A5:** Nostrils changed colors from white to purple. **B1:** Blue flower added. **B2:** Smile on lion shortened. **B3:** Belly button on alligator moved up. **C1:** Pink cheek removed from clown. **C3:** "C" changed to an "O". **D4:** Nose changed from pink to red. **D4:** Stuffed animal with blue and yellow dots changed to orange and blue dots.

Puzzle 75: Read All About It Al Fresco

A2: Slates in vent combined. **A4:** Pole removed on umbrella. **B3:** Man's head made smaller. **B4:** Pole from umbrella removed. **C3:** Earring made larger. **C3:** Collar changed color from gray to blue. **C3:** Lettering on sunglasses changed color. **C4:** Man's shirt changed color from green to maroon. **C4:** Water bottle made smaller. **E1:** Part of brown wall removed.

Puzzle 76: Make It Work — STAT!

C1: Part of tail rotor blade missing. **C2:** Cross changed color from white to yellow. **C4:** Lettering on helicopter blocked in pink. **C5:** Pilot's helmet changed color from white to yellow. **D2:** Red stripe missing. **D3:** Post made taller. **D3:** Logo added to helicopter. **D4:** Lettering on helicopter reversed. **D4:** White on back of pilot changed to yellow. **E1:** End added to railing.

Puzzle 77: Architecture with Inspiration

B2: Roof color changed from tan to blue. **B3:** Tan color added to roof. **B4:** Row of windows missing. **C4:** Two windows combined. **C5:** Row of windows added. **D1:** Shrub added. **D2:** Electrical box made larger. **D2:** Electrical equipment missing. **D3:** Rock moved. **E1:** Part of broken wall removed.

Puzzle 78: All Revved Up

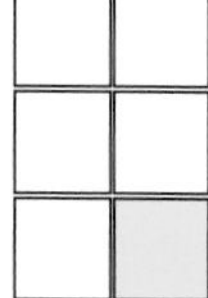

Bolt removed.

Puzzle 79: Living on the Edge

6	3	5	11
10	4	7	9
12	2	8	1

Puzzle 80: A Colorful Cavalcade of Containers

A5: Basket added. **B4:** Orange basket changed to red. **C2:** Yellow label added to broom. **C5:** Broken grid on red basket. **D3:** White label added to plastic box. **E2:** Concrete step extended. **E2:** Broom handle lengthened. **E4:** Missing part of bike sprocket. **E5:** White spout removed from green container.

Puzzle 81: Peering over Navy Pier

A5: Building shortened. **B1:** Top of building removed. **B3:** Middle disc of Ferris wheel larger. **C1:** Windows changed so that interior of building shows. **C2:** Blue disc on top of ride is now orange. **C3:** SHAKESPEARE sign reads SHAEKSPEARE. **D1:** Flag added that blocks the NAVY PIER PARK sign. **D2:** Missing blue umbrella. **D2:** Large window of trailer is smaller. **D5:** Row of windows changed to a row of trim. **D5:** Sign removed from above striped awning. **E2:** Ladder added to side of pier. **E3:** Tree stump shortened. **E4:** Part of boat name missing.

Puzzle 82: If Walls Could Talk

A1: Stone beam added to ceiling. **B2 and B3:** Black triangles changed to black diamonds. **C2:** Stems added to branch hieroglyphic. **C2 and C3:** Crack opening moved. **C4:** Branch added to hieroglyphic. **C5:** Deer hieroglyphic added. **D5:** Hieroglyphic moved lower. **D1 and E1:** Mirror image of hieroglyphic of man holding a branch. **E5:** White stripe added.

Puzzle 83: No Horsin' Around

8	1	6	11
10	3	9	2
4	5	7	12

Puzzle 84: Angles and Architecture

3	10	5	2
12	6	4	7
1	9	11	8

Puzzle 85: Sticks and Stones . . .

A2: Sea shell added. **A5:** Purple rock added. **B1:** Tan rock removed. **B5:** Small rock removed from larger rock. **C4:** Twig made shorter. **D4:** Small white rock added. **E1:** Rock enlarged. **E5:** Large rock changed color.

Puzzle 86: Up, Up, and Away!

A2: Reflected row of windows added. **A3:** Middle arch extends to top of building's right side. **B2:** Blue strip of windows changed to dark blue. **B3:** Red ball on crane missing. **C3:** Tan color reflection added to windows. **C5:** Name on crane smaller size. **C5:** Building height added. **D2:** Dark reflection added a window. **D3:** Extra window added. **D5:** Streetlight is larger. **D5:** Red removed from window. **D5:** Sign HOTEL is changed to HOTOL. **E1:** Building changed color. **E5:** Extra window added.

Puzzle 87: A Colorful Carnival Landscape

C2: Blue and white globe added. **C2:** Triangle rock enlarged. **C3:** Tent changed color from pink to purple. **C5:** Sign made longer. **C5:** Truck changed color from white to orange. **D1:** Person added. **D2:** Part on ride changed from red to blue. **E1:** Boy in red shirt missing. **E5:** 3 on sign changed to 8.

Puzzle 88: Mmm, Mmm, Good!

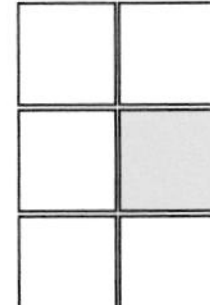

Added dot to flower on bonnet.

Puzzle 89: Speed Trap

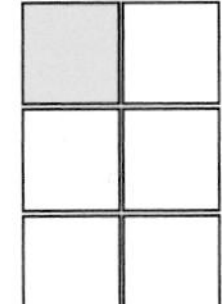

MPH is flipped to a mirror image.

Puzzle 90: One Man's Trash . . .

A1: Building extended so tree view is blocked above and directly below corrugated roof. **A5:** Missing handle to hanging bag. **B2:** Box added to stack in doorway. **B3:** Missing hammock strings. **C5:** Rolled rug is shorter. **C5:** Missing white ring from picture. **D1:** Missing grain in wood beam. **D3:** Missing last line of writing on box. **E2:** Missing rock. **E4:** Wood added to front of wood beam.

Puzzle 91: A Room with a View

A3: Pole from rooftop removed. **B1:** Window added. **B4:** Double-paned window changed to single pane. **B4:** Bird removed from top of light. **B5:** Poles on ship and treetops in background lengthened. **C3:** White decorative element between windows removed. **C4:** Speaker from pole removed. **E2:** Top of head removed. **E3:** Watermark on wooden pole shortened. **E3:** Basement window added to building. **E3:** Wooden pole shortened. **E5:** Pipe removed from side of boat.

Puzzle 92: Views from the Valley

B1: Trees added. **B5:** Windows added. **B5:** Half window made full. **C3:** Window panes on roof removed. **C3:** Triangle roof added. **D1:** Erosion netting removed. **D4:** Missing rock formation. **D5:** Opening in brick wall is removed. **E3:** L-shaped wood made larger. **E4:** Spindle added to railing.

Puzzle 93: Botanical Beauties

A3: Screw added to window frame. **A5:** Vines added to pole. **B4:** Screw removed from window frame. **C1 and C2:** Flowers changed. **C2:** Flower added. **D5:** Flower added. **D5:** Flower added. **E4:** Leaf added. **E5:** Pot increased in size.

Puzzle 94: Switches in the Swatches

A2: Two white dots filled in with color. **A4:** Design changed color from black to white. **B1:** Fabric swatch/pattern changed. **B3:** Petal added to design. **C2:** Berry added to stem on design. **D4 and D5:** Four solid dots are now opened with a lighter color. **D5:** Flower smaller. **E2:** White stripe has a darker stripe added on top of it. **E3:** Smaller flower design changed to upside-down, heartlike design.

Puzzle 95: Mountain Town

B4: Light lamp enlarged. **B4:** Telephone pole made shorter. **B5:** Stop light moved over to the left. **C2:** Words on sign reversed. **C5:** Closed windows added. **C5:** Arrow on sign moved. **D2:** White sign added. **E2:** Dog removed. **E3:** Trash can added. **E4:** Headlight added to vehicle.

Puzzle 96: Three Fair Maidens

A4: Flag removed. **A4:** Finial removed from flagpole. **B3:** Glasses changed to sunglasses. **C1:** Ferris wheel car is larger. **C4:** Pole missing. **D4:** Buckle for purse strap is shorter. **E1:** Woman's hair is longer. **E1:** Woman's shirt is longer. **E3:** Charm added to purse.

Puzzle 97: Kooky, Spooky Castle

A5: Extra bricks are added. **B4:** Planter is made larger. **B4:** Two window panes made larger. **C2:** Hair piece missing off girl. **C2:** Eyes and mouth are closed. **C4:** Part of design on railing is missing. **D2:** Crest on girl's shirt missing. **D5:** Design added on railing. **E1:** Pattern changed on bag.

Puzzle 98: Hills and High Places

C2: Peak on roof missing. **C4:** Window missing on roof. **D1:** Pole is made longer. **D2:** White column on building added. **D3:** Car added. **D3:** Van moved. **D4:** Window blinds are open. **D4:** Doorway is closed. **E2:** Parking line is missing. **E4:** Tree is added.

Puzzle 99: Purr-fectly Poised

A2: Electrical outlet added. **A2:** Dark patch near cat's eye removed. **A3:** Pattern removed from fabric. **A5:** Leaf is larger. **A5:** Cat is taller. **B1:** Outlet removed. **B4:** Cat's mouth is closed. **B4:** Leaf hanging down from pot removed. **C4:** Cat's eye color is darkened. **D1:** Potted plant is larger.

Puzzle 100: Neighborhood Watch

7	5
4	6
1	3
2	8

Part IV

The Part of Tens

"That's 3 'Genius Level Puzzle Books' at $8.95 each. Okay, I'll give you a $20, two $5s and 19¢. No wait, I'll give you two $20s and a dime, and you give me a nickel back... no, I'll keep the nickel and give you 11¢ plus the two $10s and a $20... no, wait..."

In this part . . .

No *For Dummies* book would be complete without a Part of Tens. In this part, you can find two fun chapters created in a top ten–list format. We've kept them short and sweet, giving you the skinny on the best tips for solving picture puzzles as well as ideas on how to amp up your brain power to solve puzzles better and quicker.

Chapter 2

Ten Tips for Solving

In This Chapter

- Putting a plan together and mapping out a routine
- Blocking distractions to focus on details
- Giving everything (but quitting) a try

Aw, come on — don't be embarrassed that you flipped to this chapter! Wanna know a secret? No matter how adept a puzzler, most puzzlers can't resist the temptation to flip to the tips chapter. Who wouldn't want an edge? Whether you're stumped, stuck at a certain level, or simply want to increase how quickly you solve picture puzzles, you can find some great ideas to improve your game — regardless of what kind of puzzle you're solving— in this chapter.

Getting Organized

Don't worry. When we tell you to get organized, we're not wanting you to start cleaning out closets and filling every available plastic tub with whatever odds and ends that you find. Of course, if doing so helps you solve puzzles, be our guest! On the other hand, to get geared up to solve a picture puzzle, clear the clutter from your mind, not your closet, and get yourself organized before you dive in. Being organized — whether you simply stick to a specific solving routine (which we recommend in the next section) or sit in your lucky chair with your lucky pencil and lucky cup of coffee — means getting yourself to a place where you can relax and focus on solving the puzzle.

You can find a rare breed of folks walking around who can simply flip open a puzzle book and begin solving puzzles with no organization, but if you want to feel the calm serenity that solving puzzles can bring, just get organized!

Establishing a Solving Routine

Routine is a good thing. Now say that over and over again in your head until the idea becomes, well, routine. Having a solving routine not only gives you a pattern to follow so that you don't miss any details, but it also builds your confidence as you begin to solve puzzles smarter and faster.

Some people get pretty detailed with their routine. They know exactly what time, where, and under what conditions they'll sit down and work a puzzle. If you want to add those kinds of parameters to your solving routine, that's fine, but you need to focus on establishing a routine for actually solving the puzzle itself. Nothing will frustrate you and your brain more than hopping all over a picture looking for changes or skipping from one fragment of a cut-up puzzle to another trying to randomly see whether something clicks.

Instead, decide — before you sit down to solve — exactly how you plan on solving the puzzle. For example, if you're tackling a spot-the-changes puzzle, try going from left to right, starting at the top and working your way to the bottom. Or try working it by sections in an orderly fashion (A1, A2, and so on, or A1, B1, and so on). Then again, you may find that a couple of a different strategies put together work best for you, such as, glancing through the puzzle quickly for obvious things and then setting off on a strict pattern search. Regardless of what you choose, find a routine you can stick to, which will ensure that you don't miss a thing while solving. (Check out Chapter 1 for concrete ideas on routines and patterns for solving puzzles.)

Make keeping track of your progress (see the next section) part of your routine so that you don't go back over parts of the puzzle that you've already checked. Not only is redoing what you've already checked a time waster, it's also frustrating.

Keeping Track of What You've Done

Guess what? You *can* write in this book! As a matter of fact, keeping track of what you've done helps you avoid going back to that spot again. Plus, keeping track of everything in your head is hard, especially when you're checking the answers. So track your progress and make it part of your solving routine.

But what do you mark exactly? Well, that depends on the type of puzzle:

- **Spot-the-changes puzzle:** Feel free to circle changes or jot down the change and section in the margin (for example, hat changed from blue to purple in C5). Also, mark out spots you keep going back to where you know *for sure* there aren't any changes.

- **One-of-these-is-not-like-the-other puzzle:** Unlike spot-the-changes puzzles, you're looking for just one difference in just one picture. So as you find elements that match in all of the pictures, put an X over them so that you don't drift back to those elements. For example, after you conclude that the single flower in the vase is the same color in all of the pictures, mark it. (Just be sure that all parts of that flower match . . . not just the petals!) Mark the similarities that all pictures share in just one picture rather than in all of them. Use that one picture as your checklist of all the places you've looked.
- **Cut-up puzzle:** You may find it helpful to roughly sketch next to certain pieces (you don't have to be an artist to do this) to make sure certain parts do match up. Then as you figure out which piece goes where, put a checkmark above the piece so that you know you've used it. You don't want to put a mark through the piece because you still need to look at it to figure out what other pieces connect to it.

Always use pencil. You won't be happy if you make a mistake in ink and cover up a piece of the puzzle you need to be looking at!

Limiting Distractions

Sounds obvious, we know . . . but if you find yourself having trouble staying focused on the puzzle, you may be swamped with too many distractions. Of course, life is full of distractions, but you can limit those distractions without making your partner put the TV on mute all night.

Cutting down on distractions is simply a matter of timing. Know at what times you solve puzzles the best and encounter the least amount of distractions. For example, when you're hosting a play date, you have your plate full of distractions. On the other hand, when the sugar high has worn off and the kids take a nap, you have the perfect, distraction-free chunk of time for solving puzzles.

Life's interruptions can have you wondering, "Where was I?" when you're solving a puzzle, but if you have a routine (see "Establishing a Solving Routine," earlier in this chapter), you can confidently find where you left off even if you *do* lose focus.

Scanning the Forest . . .

Taking a glance at the big picture works well when you use it as an initial strategy in your solving routine as well as when you need a break from detailed solving. Often, regardless of how great your solving routine is, and no matter if you've already scanned the entire picture earlier in your routine, you might need to switch strategies. (If you're wondering what in the world a solving routine is, see the section, "Establishing a Solving Routine," earlier in this chapter.)

So before you begin and whenever you feel stuck, take note of where you've left off, take a step back, and just check over the big picture. After you've been solving for details, you'll be amazed at how taking a step back can garner great results. When you become so familiar with details in a puzzle, foraging at the forest level can make differences (or similarities, if you're trying to piece a picture together) more obvious than if you continue poking through the plants.

. . . Scouring the Trees

Perhaps you have a solid solving routine (if not, see "Establishing a Solving Routine," earlier in this chapter), but you don't think you're getting down to the nitty-gritty details. Trust us, you can easily get lost in the details of a puzzle no matter how brilliant a solving routine you use. Really, truly seeing the trees rather than the forest involves purposefully moving through specific details within your routine.

You can purposefully move from detail to detail by repeating — in your mind or out loud — the specifics of the detail. So rather than seeing a sock on someone's foot, say to yourself, "There's a pink, knee-high sock." If you're solving a spot-the-changes or one-of-these-is-not-like-the-other puzzle, glance over at the other picture/s, while repeating the details and check whether that same sock is pink, or if it's shorter or longer. If you're piecing a picture together, look for more leg or a matching sock in a different piece. No matter what strategy or solving routine you have, pointing out the specific details of each piece of each puzzle helps you completely check through each part of the puzzle.

Trying a New Strategy

If you find yourself flipping out or frustrated because you're so close to solving a puzzle but can't quite get it done, you need to try a new strategy. Gasp! A *new* strategy? But haven't we been praising the usefulness of a solving routine? Well, yes, but sometimes you complete your routine, and you're still close to solving the puzzle, but not quite done. Then what do you do?

You could start your routine all over again, but that approach may sound tedious when you're so close to being done. If you have your wits about you and the stamina to go through your entire routine again, then, by all means, do it. But if you're looking for a quick fix, try something new. Something new doesn't necessarily mean a strategy you've never used. You can just pull out a strategy you use at the beginning or in the middle of your routine, such as sitting back and glancing at the big picture or simply taking a break. So if you need an edge, take a deep breath and try a strategy you haven't used lately.

If you try out a new strategy, don't quit halfway through. Stick it out. For example, if you decide to look at all the details of the tree trunks in a picture, don't stop if you haven't come up with anything after checking through just half of the tree trunks. After you do a few puzzles, you'll find one or two new strategies that you most often like to pull out of your back pocket when you need a fresh look.

Taking a Break . . . But Don't Quit!

Everybody needs a break sometime, so don't feel guilty about taking one no matter how close you are to getting the puzzle solved. We all take them! Especially if you think you're about to give up and just check the answers instead of completely solving the puzzle, please get up and take a break. Checking the answers prematurely can make you become more frustrated — especially when you kick yourself for how easy the answer seems — and there's simply no fun in quitting anyway.

So, when you need a break, take any kind of break you want to. Perhaps you just get up and make a fresh pot of coffee, and that activity gives you enough time away from the puzzle to sit back down and give it a fresh look. On the other hand, you may need to take a walk around the block, take a nap, or just put that puzzle down until tomorrow. Regardless of what you decide to do, when you're up against a wall, don't quit — instead, just give your mind a break.

Wrangling out of a Rut

You can find yourself spinning your wheels at the beginning of solving, in the middle, or near the end . . . basically, you can get stuck in a rut anytime. Well, don't fret because the following list gives you several things you can do — many of which we discuss in this chapter — to get yourself out of a solving rut:

- **Use a routine.** If you establish a routine for solving, you can build in several strategies to keep yourself moving instead of doing the same thing over and over again. (See "Establishing a Solving Routine," earlier in this chapter.)
- **Assess whether you're focused.** If you're allowing a lot of things to distract you, you need to get rid of them. (See the section earlier in this chapter, "Limiting Distractions.")

- **Check to see whether you simply need a break.** Especially if you've been solving for a while, you may just need a break. If so, take one. (See the section earlier, "Take a Break . . . But Don't Quit.")
- **Pull out a new strategy.** If you're scouring the puzzle using the same strategy over and over again, try something new. Even if you use a strategy that you used earlier in solving, it can feel new and result in a fresh outlook. (See the earlier section, "Trying a New Strategy" for more information.)

Noticing the Unnoticeable

An unnoticeable element refers to that one last piece or change that stands between you and solving the puzzle. Different from spinning your wheels in a rut or hitting a wall, the unnoticeable element simply eludes you regardless of what strategy you use. So wait! You need to first determine whether you're simply in a rut. So try out the tips in "Wrangling out of a Rut," earlier in this chapter, before you move on in this section.

If you're not just in a rut, you're likely missing a detail in a detail. If you're sure that you've checked all the elements, begin with checking out elements you've already marked off your list. (See "Keeping Track of What You've Done," earlier in this chapter.) Make sure that you didn't overlook a detail with that element. For example, you know you checked where the tree is placed and how tall it is, but did you check whether the trunk is shorter or longer or whether the branches extend as far as you thought they did?

Chapter 3

Ten Ways to Build Your Brain for Better Solving

In This Chapter

- Sharpening your focus and attention
- Using different activities to raise your solving quotient
- Keeping your body in good working order

Although you can get specific tips on solving picture puzzles (see Chapter 2), we give you the biggest solving tip right here: Work out that big muscle in your head. Maintaining focus or approaching puzzles in a new way exercises that gray matter. And in this chapter, we give you several activities and challenges that can shift your brain into a higher gear, ready and waiting to solve picture puzzles.

Keeping Your Focus

Of course, solving a puzzle in a nice, quiet space, devoid of all interruption, may be your ideal, but sometimes it's not exactly realistic. You have a life going on around you, such as children needing attention, the phone ringing, the dryer buzzer going off, or horns honking . . . wait a minute . . . you're not driving, are you? While keeping your focus can be a challenge, it can increase your puzzle-solving skills.

Making sure you stay focused in spite of interruptions takes a little preparation and practice. You know what kinds of interruptions you'll encounter, so prepare for them and practice paying no attention to those things until you've found a good stopping point. For example, if you know you're going to work a puzzle while waiting in the doctor's office, you don't want to look up every time the door opens, a name is called, or someone coughs and sneezes. So prepare for those interruptions. Don't worry — you won't miss your name being called. By the time they yell your name for the third time, you'll hear them.

By the same token, if you're at home while the kids are playing and the laundry is in the dryer, either use those interruptions for natural boundaries or build your own boundaries. Use the dryer buzzing or the kids' snack time as your signal to take a break. (Taking a break is a good thing sometimes — see the section, "Taking a Break . . . But Don't Quit!" later in this chapter.) If you know you're bound to be interrupted, prepare yourself to keep focused on the puzzle until you can note where you've stopped. Of course, if the kids are bleeding or suffering from broken bones, feel free to drop everything at once and frantically run about the house until they're mended.

Finding the Right Spot to Settle In

Ah, the comfy chair, the quiet patio, the serene library . . . you figure one of these spots should be perfect for puzzling, right? Then your chair won't recline just right, a flock of geese constantly flies over your patio, and the library has just been overrun by a group of school children. By this point, you may be wondering whether the "right spot" actually exists.

Lucky for you, defining your perfect spot for puzzling doesn't require an advanced degree. First, determine what kind of environment you need. Do you like the low murmur of a TV or radio in the background? Do you prefer absolute quiet, which may be impossible to find short of locking yourself in the bathroom? After you understand the kind of environment that suits your puzzling personality the best, just get out there and find it.

If nothing else, be flexible. You can have more than one spot. For example, if your comfy chair happens to be in the family room, and you sit down for a picture puzzle marathon at the same time that your partner wants to watch the big game, you need to change your spot. Have a backup spot . . . or two!

Engaging Your Attention

Of course, picture puzzles have plenty to tickle your attention, but you can improve your solving skills and technique by engaging your mind in other ways. Solving picture puzzles relies on keen concentration, and you can sharpen your mind simply by exercising it.

Find enjoyable activities that force you to concentrate, especially for long periods of time — even better with distractions you have to block out. Maybe you get into bird-watching and enjoy sitting still for that one moment when you see or hear a bird and seek it out, studying the bird's characteristics. On the other hand, you may be a game player who enjoys chess or bingo. Both of those games demand attention in different ways, and bingo has the bonus of having plenty of distractions. Any way you look at it, you can find an activity that appeals to you — from video games to painting — that can put your attention to the test for long periods of time.

Trying a Variety of Other Puzzles

We *do* allow you to cheat on this picture puzzle book with other puzzles. In fact, we encourage it! Pick up *Sudoku For Dummies, Crossword Puzzles For Dummies,* or *Brain Games For Dummies* (all published by Wiley) and try them out. Doing different puzzles gets your brain thinking in different ways, which can give you an edge as you solve picture puzzles.

Ever ask someone for an opinion, hoping that this person sees your issue from an angle you haven't thought of before? Well, getting your brain thinking in ways it hasn't before in regards to puzzles can give you the different angle you need to approach solving picture puzzles in a novel way. Perhaps you have trouble getting into a solving routine or sticking to one. Doing some Sudoku puzzles can definitely solidify the benefits of using a solving routine. So do some different puzzles — even if it's just the daily crossword — and you may find yourself approaching your next picture puzzle in a new way.

Taking a Break from Mind-Numbing Activities

To keep your brain in top-notch shape, skip or at least limit the habits that tend to make you veg out. Just as keeping your attention engaged in an activity or different puzzle can boost your brain power, vegging out over the latest movie rental or that season marathon of a reality show that you've seen a million times makes your brain go into a lull. Plus, television can actually shorten your attention span, whether you skip through the commercials or not.

But you can find other activities that mush your mind just as much as television does. For example, when was the last time you checked out Facebook, tweeted on Twitter, or just browsed down a rabbit hole online? Try inventorying the things you do in a few days or a week, and see how many mind-numbing activities you do and how much time it eats out of your day.

Mind-numbing activities have their place. Just don't let these activities take up too much time in your life. Whether it be your heart health or mental health, limiting mind-numbing activities — or eliminating them altogether — benefits your mind, body, and soul.

Learning Something New

You can work several different parts of your brain just by learning something new. Whether you decide to learn one foreign phrase each day or challenge yourself to learn a new skill each month, newness gets your brain going. You work your memory as well as the way in which your brain associates things. In addition, learning something new takes focus and attention, both of which help you solve picture puzzles better. Plus, learning something new is a great break from solving puzzles if you need one.

You have to practice your new skill to best influence your brain's activity. However, after you find that skill becoming routine, find something new to learn again.

Reading, Writing, and 'Rithmetic

Yep, just like your first-grade teacher told you, the three Rs keep your brain buzzing. Although all three of these activities stimulate your brain, reading challenges you to learn new words and process information. Challenge yourself to read the news rather than listen or watch it. When you have a question about something, look it up and read about it — you might just learn something new. (For more on learning new things, check out the earlier section, "Learning Something New.")

Writing encourages creativity, and you may need some creative ideas when it comes to solving bewildering picture puzzles. In addition, writing motivates you to sort things out and put things into perspective. Whether you blog, journal, or simply write a grocery list, you put mental organization into practice, not to mention remembering to get a gallon of milk.

Making the most of math during your day doesn't require you to sit down and do a math workbook. Instead, work out life's story problems. That trendy new outfit is 25 percent off. Buying in bulk may tempt you, but you need to decide whether it's truly a good deal. Figure these kinds of things out without a calculator to stimulate your problem-solving skills, which come in handy when solving problematic picture puzzles.

Clearing Your Mind

Clearing clutter from your mind frees you up to focus on other things, such as solving that picture puzzle you've been staring at for ten minutes. If you try to solve a puzzle while you also try to figure out what you need at the grocery store, put together a to-do list for tomorrow morning, and figure out how many hours have passed since you last ate, your eyes will glaze over in no time.

Free your mind from clutter before you sit down to solve a puzzle. You can best clear your head by simply jotting down the mental things that interrupt your focus and then find ways to combat those interruptions. For example, if you find yourself wanting to set up your to-do list while solving, decide to work on the to-do list first to put your mind at ease. If you worry over how much time has passed because you don't want to miss an appointment, set a timer so that you don't have to keep watching the clock.

Eating Right

We don't have a specific diet plan to put you on, but you do need to eat right for mental health, not just physical health. Make low-fat, low-cholesterol foods part of your brain-healthy diet. Whole grain foods, fruits, veggies, lean meats, and a limited amount of healthy fats work together to keep your body and brain functioning in a positive direction. And if your family and friends question a sudden change in your eating habits, let them know that you're just in training.

Too much sugar and too few *antioxidants* — vitamins and other nutrients that help protect cells from the damage of free radicals — (you can find antioxidants in foods, such as berries, broccoli, Brussels sprouts, and beets) can hamper your mental performance.

Keeping Active

Your brain benefits from lower cholesterol, a strong heart, and increased levels of oxygen in your blood. You can achieve such things through physical activity. Get some fresh air, get your blood circulating and your heart pumping (but not too hard), and stay active. As you increase your physical health, your mental health benefits as well.

By no means do we mean for you to stay up all day and night, putting into practice the tips and advice we've given you in this book. Keep active in a physical way, but don't stay active 24 hours a day . . . or even 20. Both your brain and your body need rest to recharge and to think straight so get some sleep!